Key Stage 3

Science

Summary and Practice Book

Name	Cavan Holsgrove
School	Depford green
Class / Set	9y2

How to use this book

This book has been carefully designed to help you to prepare for the national Key Stage 3 Tests that all students do in Year 9.

You will take the Tests at one of the two 'tiers'. The Lower Tier covers Levels 3–6 of the National Curriculum.
The Higher Tier covers Levels 5–7.
This book gives you practice for both of these tiers.

The book covers the National Curriculum in short clear topics.
There are 7 topics for each of Biology, Chemistry and Physics, as shown in the Contents list (on page 4).
Each topic is laid out as a group of three double-page spreads.
The diagrams on the opposite page show you the layout of these spreads.

On the opposite page, you should read numbers **1** to **12** carefully, to see how the book has been designed to help you to revise and practise your Science.

When answering the questions, you can write your answers on this book, or write them on a sheet of paper. Your teacher will tell you which method to use.
If you need to look at the QuickTest **Answers** (on page 140), make sure that you use them to learn and understand the correct answer.

The Questions on **Paper A** (Levels 3–6) and **Paper B** (Levels 5–7) are all the same style as the national Test, so you can become well prepared for the real thing.
After you have tried these Questions, your teacher can give you the correct answers if they are not included in this copy of the book. Look at these carefully to see where you may have lost marks, so you can do better next time.

At the back of the book is a **Glossary**. This explains the meaning of important scientific words that you need to understand.

We hope you will find this book very helpful in preparing yourself for the Tests.

Keith Johnson
Sue Adamson
Gareth Williams

Each of the 21 topics has 3 parts:

Each topic begins like this:

Each topic is clearly labelled and colour coded.

A photo or diagram sets the scene.

A clear summary of **What you need to know** on this topic, to cover the National Curriculum.

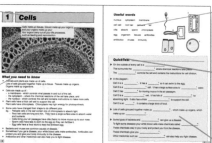

4 A list of **Useful Words**, with a diagram. These are to help you with the QuickTest.

5 A **QuickTest** to test yourself by filling in the missing words. Read the Useful Words if you need help.

6 If you get stuck, the **Answers** are on page 141.

The second part of each topic:

A double-page of **Questions at Levels 3–6**, for the Lower Tier.

The Questions are all in the same style as the national Test that you will take in Year 9. You should try to do all of them.

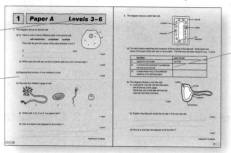

9 Your teacher will tell you whether to write your answers on this book, or on paper.

The third part of each topic:

A double-page spread of **Questions at Levels 5–7**. Try to do as many of them as you can.

If you are to be entered at this Higher Tier, you should first also do the Questions at Level 3–6.

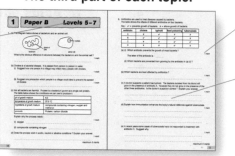

11 The **marks** are shown for each question, just like in the real Test.

12 If you have the Answers version of this book, the answers are at the back. Or your teacher can give you the correct answers.

Contents

Biology

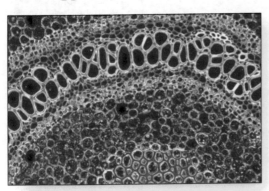

Chemistry

Physics

1 Cells

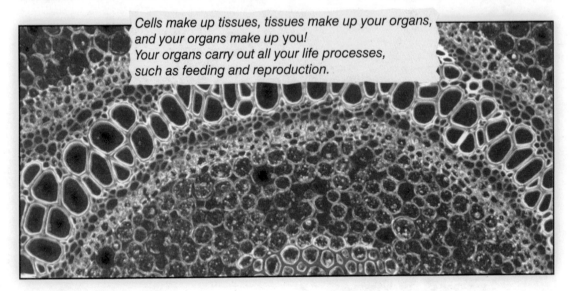

Cells make up tissues, tissues make up your organs, and your organs make up you!
Your organs carry out all your life processes, such as feeding and reproduction.

What you need to know

- Animals and plants are made up of cells.
  Lots of cells grouped together make up a tissue. Tissues make up organs.
  Organs make up organisms.

- Cells are made up of :
  - a membrane – which controls what passes in and out of the cell,
  - the cytoplasm – where the chemical reactions of the cell take place, and
  - the nucleus – which controls the cell and contains instructions to make more cells.
- Plant cells have a thick cell wall to support the cell.
  Plant cells have chloroplasts. Chloroplasts trap light energy for photosynthesis.

- Some cells have changed their shape to do different jobs
  eg. – Cells lining your air passages have cilia (hairs) to move mucus up to your nose.
  - Sperm cells have tails to swim to the egg so they can fertilise it.
  - Egg cells have a food store to feed the fertilised egg.
  - Root hair cells are long and thin. They have a large surface area to absorb water and nutrients.
  - Palisade cells in the leaf contain lots of chloroplasts to absorb light.

- Bacteria and viruses can grow and reproduce inside your body. They are a common cause of disease.
- Sometimes if you get a disease, your white blood cells make antibodies. Antibodies can protect you and give your body immunity to the disease.
- Antibiotics and other medicines can also help you to fight disease.

Useful words

nucleus   cytoplasm   membrane

cell wall   root hair   palisade   tail

cilia   absorb   sperm   chloroplasts

egg   organism   tissues   antibodies

antibiotics   viruses   immunity

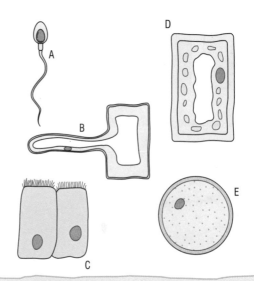

QuickTest...

▶ On the outside of every cell is a _____ [1].

This surrounds the _____ [2] where chemical reactions take place.

The _____ [3] controls the cell and contains the instructions for cell division.

▶ In the diagram :

Cell A is a _____ [4], it has a _____ [5] so it can swim to the egg.

Cell B is a _____ [6] cell. It has a large surface area to _____ [7] water.

Cell C has _____ [8] for moving mucus in the air passages.

Cell D is a _____ [9] cell. It has lots of _____ [10] for

absorbing light. It also has a thick _____ [11] to support the cell.

Cell E is an _____ [12] . It contains a large store of food.

▶ Lots of cells grouped together make up _____ [13] , which make up organs, which

make up an _____ [14] .

▶ Some types of bacteria and _____ [15] can give us a disease.

To fight some diseases your white blood cells make chemicals called _____ [16] .

These chemicals stay in your body and protect you from the disease.

These chemicals give you _____ [17] .

Other medicines such as _____ [18] can also help you fight disease.

1. The diagram shows an animal cell.

(a) (i) Here is a list of some different parts of an animal cell.

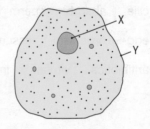

cell membrane   cytoplasm   nucleus

From this list give the name of the parts labelled X and Y.

X _____ and

Y _____

2 marks

(ii) Which part of a cell can we find in plants cells but not in animal cells ?

1 mark

_____

(b) Describe the function of the nucleus in a cell.

1 mark

_____

(c) Here are four different types of cell.

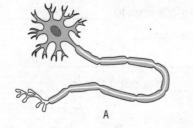

A   B   C   D

(i) Which cell, A, B, C or D, is a sperm cell ?

1 mark

_____

(ii) How is a sperm cell adapted to its function ?

1 mark

_____

_____

maximum 6 marks

2. The diagram shows a plant leaf cell.

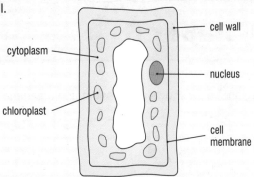

(a) The table below describes the functions of three parts of the leaf cell. Write down the name of the part of the cell next to its function. The first one has been done for you. *2 marks*

	function	part of cell
(i)	it gives the cell shape	cell wall
(ii)	it controls the movement of substances into and out of the cell	
(iii)	a place where many of the chemical reactions of the cell take place	

(b) The diagram shows a root hair cell.

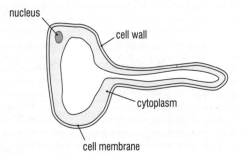

(i) Look at the root hair cell and the plant cell at the top of the page.
Name the part of the leaf cell that the root hair cell does not have.

_____
1 mark

(ii) Explain why this part would be no use in the root hair cell.

1 mark

_____

_____

(iii) How is a root hair cell adapted to its function ?

1 mark

_____

maximum 5 marks

Paper B   Levels 5–7

1. (a) The diagram below shows a bacterium and an animal cell.

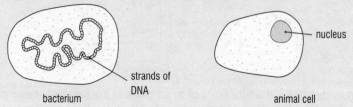

bacterium

strands of DNA

animal cell

nucleus

What is the obvious difference in structure between the bacterium and the animal cell ?

1 mark

_____

(b) Cholera is a bacterial disease. It is passed from person to person in water.
   (i) Suggest how one person in a village may infect many people with cholera.

1 mark

_____

   (ii) Suggest one precaution which people in a village could take to prevent the spread of cholera

1 mark

_____

(c) Not all bacteria are harmful. Pruteen is a bacterium grown as a single cell protein. The table below shows the conditions we can use to produce it.

pH of growth medium	6.0
temperature of growth medium	37.5 °C
ingredients of growth medium	compounds containing nitrogen, oxygen and methanol
products	Pruteen; carbon dioxide

Explain why the process needs :

1 mark

(i) oxygen _____

1 mark

(ii) compounds containing nitrogen _____

(d) Does the process work in acidic, neutral or alkaline conditions ? Explain your answer.

1 mark

_____

maximum 6 marks

2. Antibiotics are used to treat diseases caused by bacteria.
The table shows the effects of different antibiotics on four bacteria.

Key : ✔ = prevents growth of bacteria   ✘ = allows growth of bacteria

antibiotic	cholera	typhoid	food poisoning	tuberculosis
A	✘	✔	✘	✘
B	✔	✔	✔	✘
C	✘	✘	✔	✔
D	✘	✘	✔	✘

(a) (i) Which antibiotic prevents the growth of most bacteria ?

1 mark

The letter of the antibiotic is : _____

(ii) Which bacteria are prevented from growing by the antibiotic in (a) (i) ?

1 mark

_____

(b) Which bacteria are least affected by antibiotics ?

1 mark

_____

(c) A doctor suspects a patient has typhoid. The bacteria isolated from his blood will
grow in the presence of antibiotic A. However they do not grow in the presence of the
other three antibiotics. Is the doctor's suspicion correct ? Explain your answer.

1 mark

_____

_____

(d) Explain how immunisation enhances the body's natural defences against tuberculosis.

2 marks

_____

_____

_____

(e) In recent years some cases of tuberculosis have not responded to treatment with
antibiotic C. Suggest why.

1 mark

_____

_____

maximum 7 marks

2 Food and digestion

You need food for energy and for growth. Without the right sort of food you won't grow strong and healthy.

What you need to know

- A healthy diet has a variety of foods, each in the right amount.
- A balanced diet contains carbohydrates, proteins, fats, minerals, vitamins, fibre and water.

- Carbohydrates and fats are used as fuel in our bodies.
  During respiration they release energy.
- Sugary and starchy foods are a good source of carbohydrate. Vegetable oils are a good source of fats.
- Proteins are needed for growth. We use them to make new cells and to repair damaged tissue.
- Fish and lean meat and seeds are rich in protein.
- We need small amounts of vitamin A, vitamin B group, vitamin C, iron and calcium to stay healthy.

- Fibre is needed to help pass food along our gut.
  Foods like cereals and vegetables have lots of fibre.
- We must digest our food before our bodies can use it.
  Digestion means breaking down large, insoluble molecules into small, soluble molecules.
- Enzymes can digest large food molecules like starch, proteins and fats.
- Food has to be digested if it is to pass through the gut wall and get into the blood.
- Indigestible material is egested (passed out) from the gut as waste.

- Alcohol abuse can affect a person's lifestyle, family and health.
- Abuse of solvents and other drugs can affect your health.

Useful words

fibre   carbohydrates   balanced

proteins   vitamins   fats   minerals

respiration   digestion   enzymes

insoluble   blood   egestion   gut

solvents   alcohol

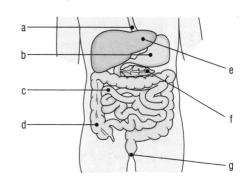

QuickTest ....

▶ A _____ [1] diet contains all the right foods in the correct amounts.

Your body's main fuels are _____ [2] and _____ [3].

These are needed to release energy during _____ [4].

You need _____ [5] for growth and repair of cells and tissues.

In order to stay healthy you need _____ [6] and _____ [7] in small amounts.

You need _____ [8] to add bulk to your food. It helps the muscles of the gut wall

to squeeze the food along.

▶ Our food is made up of large, _____ [9] molecules. We have to break it down

into small soluble molecules before we can use it. This is called _____ [10].

To do this we make chemicals called _____ [11]. The large molecules are cut up into

smaller ones by the _____ [12].

▶ The products of _____ [13] pass through the _____ [14] wall into the _____ [15].

Indigestible food passes out of the _____ [16] as waste. This is called _____ [17].

▶ Abuse of _____ [18] can be addictive and harm a person's health.

_____ [19] and other drugs can also have harmful effects on the body.

▶ Look at the diagram of the gut.

Use these words to complete the labels :

| stomach   small intestine   anus   gullet |
| liver   pancreas   large intestine |

a. _____ [20]   b. _____ [21]   c. _____ _____ [22]

d. _____ _____ [23]   e. _____ [24]   f. _____ [25]   g. _____ [26]

13

1. A balanced diet contains a variety of foods which give us nutrients and energy.
The drawings show four foods.

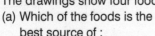  

lamb	orange	milk	crisps

(a) Which of the foods is the best source of :

(i) calcium ? _____

(ii) vitamin C ? _____

(iii) protein ? _____

3 marks

(b) Name **one** other group of substances, apart from protein, which we need for a healthy diet. Give one reason why we need this group of substances.

1 mark

Group of substances _____

We need this group of substances to _____

1 mark

(c) Why do we need fibre for a balanced diet ?

1 mark

_____

The bar chart shows the recommended daily amounts of calcium for different age groups of people.

(d) The amount of calcium a man needs is least when he is fully grown. Explain why.

1 mark

_____

_____

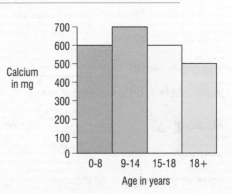

Calcium in mg

(e) Explain why a mother needs 1200 mg of calcium each day when she is breast-feeding a baby.

1 mark

_____

_____

maximum 8 marks

2. (a) Some health problems are caused by an unbalanced diet.
Match each health problem to its cause.   *1 mark*

health problem   cause

| overweight |

| tooth decay |

| anaemia |

| not enough iron |

| too much fatty food |

| too many sweets |

(b) Some of the different groups of substances in food are :

carbohydrates   fats   mineral salts   proteins   vitamins

Which of these groups of substances :
                                                                          1 mark
(i) is used by the body for growth and repair; _____

(ii) are main sources of energy for the body ? _____ and
                                                                          1 mark

_____

(c) The diagram shows part of the human body.

Identify **two** parts of the body where
digestion occurs.   *2 marks*

(d) Name the group of chemicals in the body
which help to digest our food.

_____   *1 mark*

(e) During digestion large molecules found in
food are broken down into smaller
molecules.
Why is this necessary ?

                                                                          1 mark

_____

_____

_____

                                                    maximum 7 marks

1. Carbohydrates, fats and proteins are three groups of nutrients.
    (a) Name **two** other **types** of nutrients that we need for a balanced diet.

    2 marks

    1 _____ 2 _____

The contents of some foods
are shown in the table.

foods	carbohydrate %	fat %	protein %
carrots	5.40	0.00	0.70
orange	8.50	0.00	0.80
beef	0.00	28.20	14.80
herring	0.00	14.10	16.00
bread	54.60	1.70	8.30
rice	86.80	1.00	6.20

(b) Which food contains most of the nutrient used by the body for growth and repair ?

1 mark

_____

(c) Fibre is not digested but it is an important part of a balanced diet.
    Which food in the table would contain the most fibre ?

1 mark

_____

(d) Dairy products are an important group of foods.

1 mark

Name **one** dairy product not given in the table _____

Name a nutrient which this food contains _____

(e) Here is some information about the amount of energy produced by foods in the body.
    1 g of carbohydrate produces 16 kJ
    1 g of fat produces 38 kJ
    1 g of protein produces 17 kJ
    Use this information to calculate the maximum amount of energy which could be
    produced in the body by eating 100 g of carrots.

1 mark

_____

maximum 6 marks

2. Look at the pie charts . They show the proportion by mass of various foods in the diets of people from countries in three different parts of the world.

Africa   South America   Asia

☐ Cereals
■ Fruit, Vegetables
☐ Meat, Fish, Eggs
☐ Dairy foods

(a) In which part of the world does food of animal origin form the largest part of the diet ?

1 mark

_____

(b) In South America the average daily intake of food is 1600 g.
Approximately how much of this is made up of cereals ?

1 mark

_____

(c) In Asia people eat more fruits, vegetables and cereals than in Britain
In Asia cancer of the intestine is much less common than in Britain.
Suggest which food group is present in these types of food and explain how it may help in the intestine.

1 mark

The food component is _____

In the intestine it _____

(d) In 1896 a Dutch doctor working in Asia was searching for the cause of a disease called beri beri.
He fed two groups of hens as follows:
Group A– rice which had the husks removed
Group B – rice that had the husks left on
He found that the hens in Group A developed beriberi but the hens in Group B were healthy. He also found that the hens in Group A could be cured by feeding them rice which had the husks left on.

(i) Give two factors the doctor would need to control to make this a fair test.   *2 marks*

1 _____

2 _____

(ii) At the start of the experiment the doctor thought that beri beri was caused by a germ.
Explain whether this was supported or not by the results of the experiment.   *1 mark*

(iii) We now know that beri beri is caused by a lack of small amounts of nutrients in the diet. What sort of nutrients ?
1 mark

_____

maximum 7 marks

3 The active body

*We need to exercise if we are
to lead fit, active lives.
Exercise keeps our lungs, heart
and muscles healthy.*

What you need to know

- Oxygen is used in your cells to release energy from food. This is called respiration.
  oxygen + glucose → carbon dioxide + water + energy
- During respiration, glucose is broken down into carbon dioxide and water.

- Air gets to the air sacs of your lungs through the wind-pipe and air passages.
- Oxygen passes through the air sacs into the blood capillaries.
  Carbon dioxide passes the opposite way, from the blood capillaries
  into the air sacs.

- Tobacco smoke contains harmful chemicals that can damage your lungs.
  It causes diseases such as lung cancer, bronchitis and heart disease.

- Your blood transports the oxygen and dissolved food as well as
  carbon dioxide and other waste chemicals around your body.
  Food and oxygen pass out of the blood capillaries into the cells.
  Carbon dioxide and other waste chemicals pass in the opposite direction.

- Your skeleton supports and protects your body and allows you to move.
- Your muscles provide the force needed to move bones at joints.
- When one muscle in a pair contracts, the other one relaxes. We say that
  they are antagonistic.

Useful words

oxygen   carbon dioxide

respiration   wind-pipe

energy   blood   food

bronchitis   cancer

lungs   kidneys

joints   bones

skeleton   protects

antagonistic   contracts

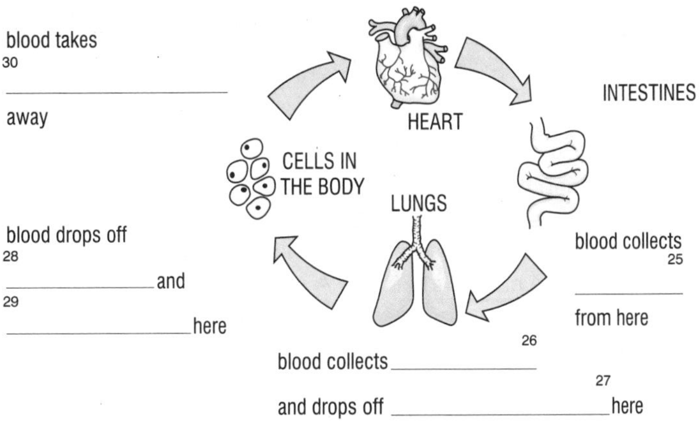

blood takes
30
_____
away

blood drops off
28
_____ and
29
_____ here

CELLS IN
THE BODY

HEART

LUNGS

INTESTINES

blood collects
25
_____
from here

blood collects _____
26
27
and drops off _____ here

QuickTest ....

▶ During _____ [1] glucose is broken down in the cells to release

_____ [2]. The gas _____ [3] is needed for this to happen.

As the glucose is broken down, _____ [4] and water are produced.

This process is called _____ [5]. It takes place in all the cells of your body.

▶ Your _____ [6] are made up of millions of tiny air sacs.

Air reaches the air sacs through the _____ [7] and air passages.

_____ [8] gas passes through the air sacs into the _____ [9] in the capillaries.

_____ [10] gas passes from the capillaries into the air sacs.

▶ Your _____ [11] carries _____ [12] from your lungs to the tissues, and

_____ [13] from the tissues to your _____ [14].

Your _____ [15] also transports dissolved _____ [16] from your gut and waste

chemicals to your _____ [17].

▶ Smoking can cause serious diseases such as lung _____ [18] and

_____ [19].

▶ Your _____ [20] supports and _____ [21] your body and enables you to move.

Muscles move _____ [22] at joints. When one muscle in a pair _____ [23],

the other one relaxes. We say that these muscles are _____ [24].

▶ Look at the diagram above. Use some of the useful words to fill in the gaps.

1. The human body has organs. Each of these has a different function.

(a) The picture shows part of the human body. Write the names of organs A and B.

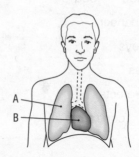

1 mark

A is the _____

1 mark

B is the _____

(b) Complete the following table.

2 marks

organ system	function in the body
circulatory system	
	absorbs oxygen from the air into the blood and expels carbon dioxide

(c) Respiration is the process by which energy is released in the body. Complete the word equation for respiration.

1 mark

_____ + oxygen ⟹ carbon dioxide + _____

(d) The diagram opposite shows a single air sac in a lung. State two features of air sacs which make them suitable for gas exchange.

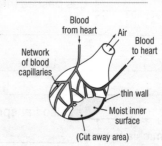

2 marks

1 _____

2 _____

(e) Air sacs occur in groups in the lungs. Heavy smokers often have coughs. Coughing breaks down the walls between the air sacs.

Suggest why heavy smokers often have to breathe very quickly even when walking slowly. *2 marks*

_____

_____

_____

maximum 9 marks

2. (a) Which mineral in food is important for the growth of bones ?

1 mark

Choose the correct answer.

calcium   A   potassium   C

iron   B   sodium   D

(b) The list below gives the names of four parts of the skeleton.

pelvis   rib cage   skull   spine

Which of these parts :

2 marks

(i)   protects the brain from damage ?   _____

(ii) is where the legs are attached ?   _____

(c) The diagram shows an arm.

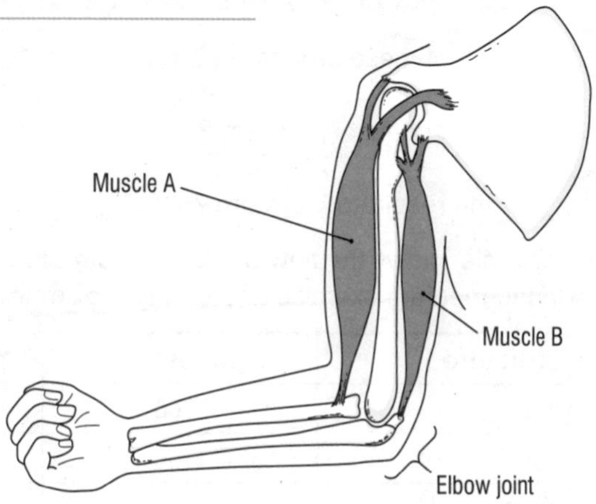

(i)   Complete the following
sentences using only the
words **contracts** or **relaxes**.

2 marks

Muscle A

Muscle B

Elbow joint

When the arm is bent at the elbow muscle A _____ and

muscle B _____ .

When the arm is straightened muscle A _____ and

muscle B _____ .

(ii) What word describes pairs of muscles like A and B which work together ?

1 mark

_____

maximum 6 marks

1. (a) The diagrams below show four organs of the human body.
   They are not drawn to the same scale.

 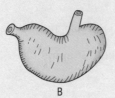 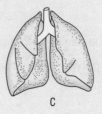 

A   B   C   D

kidney   stomach   heart   lungs

Match each of the organs shown with its name.   *4 marks*

(b) Which of these organs is part of :
                                                                           2 marks

   (i) the circulatory system ? _____

   (ii) the respiratory system ? _____

The table shows the flow of blood, in cm^3, to different parts of the body while at rest, during medium exercise and during maximum exercise.

structure	at rest	medium exercise	maximum exercise
brain	700	700	700
gut	1350	800	300
heart muscles	250	550	950
skeletal muscles	1200	8200	21 000

(c) Which structure shows no change in the rate of blood flow ? Suggest a reason for this.
                                                                           2 marks

   Structure _____

   Reason _____

(d) Explain why the rate of blood flow to the skeletal muscles changes as you exercise.
                                                                           2 marks

   _____

   _____

                                                              maximum 10 marks

2. The diagram shows a hinge joint.

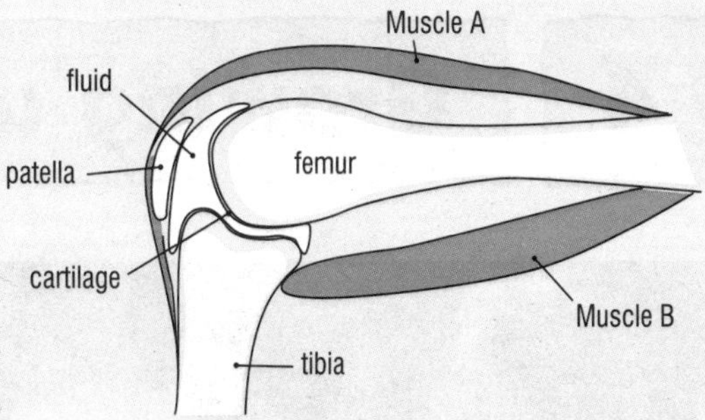

(a) In which part of the body is this joint ?

1 mark

_____

(b) Explain how muscle A and muscle B
make the bones of the joint move.

2 marks

_____

_____

_____

Arthritis is a condition which affects people's bones. Read this passage about arthritis.

Osteo-arthritis is common in elderly people. It is due to wear and tear of the joints.
The smooth cartilage breaks down and bony knobs develop on the moving surface.
Rheumatoid arthritis often runs in families. Connective tissue grows in the joints and
hardens. This makes the joint difficult to move.
Hip joints are often affected by arthritis. Replacement hip joints made out of stainless
steel (or titanium) and plastic may be fitted in place of a diseased joint.

(c) Which type of arthritis is :

2 marks

(i) hereditary ? _____

(ii) most likely to be encountered in old age ? _____

(d) How does cartilage help a normal joint to work properly ?

1 mark

_____

_____

(e) The diagram shows a replacement hip joint.

Into which parts of the body are the two parts fitted ?

1 mark

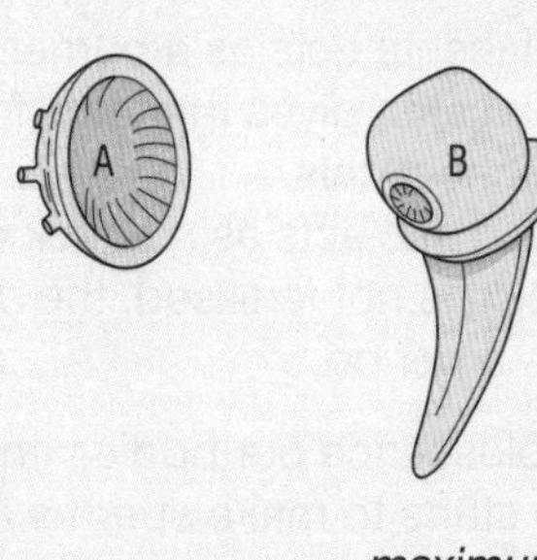

Part A _____

Part B _____

maximum 7 marks

23

4 Growing up

As we grow up, we change from a baby to a child, then to a teenager and eventually to an adult. We develop physically and mentally. Our emotions change as we mix with other people.

What you need to know

- The sperm tube carries sperm made in the testes to the penis; glands add fluid to make semen.
- The egg tube carries an egg from an ovary to the uterus every month.

- During love-making sperms are placed into the vagina.
- At fertilisation the sperm penetrates the egg and its nucleus joins with the egg nucleus.
- If the egg is fertilised it passes down the egg tube and settles into the uterus.
- The fertilised egg grows first into an embryo and then into a fetus.

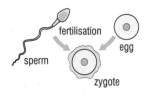

- The placenta acts as a barrier to infections and harmful substances.
- The placenta gives the fetus food and oxygen and removes carbon dioxide and other waste chemicals.
- The fluid sac acts as a shock absorber to protect the fetus.
- If an egg is not fertilised, the uterus lining breaks down and leaves through the vagina. This is a period.

- At adolescence our bodies and our emotions change.
- A boy starts to make sperms and grow body hair, and his voice deepens.
- A girl starts to make eggs, her breasts develop and she starts having periods.

Useful words

testes   semen   sperm tube

vagina   egg tube   uterus   ovaries

fertilisation   embryo   fluid sac   cord

placenta   period   adolescence

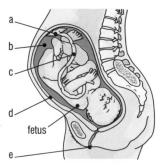

a

b

c

d

fetus

e

QuickTest ....

▶ The _____ [1] make sperms. The sperms pass along the _____ [2] to the penis.

On the way, glands add a fluid to the sperms to make _____ [3]. The _____ [4] make eggs. The egg passes along the _____ [5] towards the _____ [6].

▶ During love-making, sperms are placed inside the _____ [7].

At _____ [8] a sperm penetrates an egg in the _____ [9]. The fertilised egg passes down the _____ [10] and settles into the lining of the _____ [11].

Here the fertilised egg will grow into an _____ [12] and then into a fetus.

▶ Soon the _____ [13] forms as a barrier to protect the fetus. The _____ [14] gives the fetus food and oxygen and removes carbon dioxide and other waste chemicals.

The fetus is attached to the _____ [15] by the _____ [16].

The _____ [17] surrounds the fetus and acts as a shock absorber.

▶ If there is no fertilised egg then the lining of the _____ [18] breaks down and some blood and cells pass out of the body through the _____ [19]. This is known as a _____ [20].

At _____ [21] a boy's _____ [22] start to make sperms. He grows body hair and his voice breaks.

▶ At _____ [23] a girl's _____ [24] start to make eggs. Her breasts develop and she starts to have _____ [25].

▶ Look at the diagram. Use some of the useful words to complete the labels :

a. _____ [26]   b. _____ [27]   c. _____ [28]   d. _____ [29]   e. _____ [30]

1. The diagram shows a baby developing inside its mother's body.

   (a) In which of the labelled parts :

   2 marks

   (i) are eggs produced ?

   _____

   (ii) does the baby pass through to be born ?

   _____

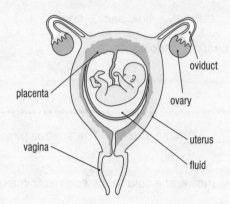

placenta

oviduct

ovary

uterus

vagina

fluid

(b) Substances are passed between the mother and baby through the placenta. Name **one** substance which passes from :

2 marks

   (i) the mother to the baby _____

   (ii) the baby to the mother _____

(c) (i) If a pregnant woman smokes cigarettes, substances can pass from the smoke to the unborn baby. These substances can affect the development of the baby's brain.

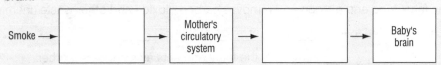

Smoke → [   ] → Mother's circulatory system → [   ] → Baby's brain

   Complete the boxes which show the path taken by these substances. *1 mark*

   (ii) Name **one** other substance which, if taken by the mother, may affect the development of the baby.

1 mark

   _____

(d) During pregnancy the baby is surrounded by fluid. State one way in which this helps the developing baby.

1 mark

_____

_____

maximum 7 marks

2. Here are four stages in human reproduction.

ovulation ⇒ fertilisation ⇒ gestation ⇒ birth

(a) How long is it normally between ovulation and the birth ?

1 mark

Choose the correct answer.

| 20 weeks | A | | 40 weeks | C |
| 30 weeks | B | | 50 weeks | D |

(b) In which **one** of the following does fertilisation normally take place ?

1 mark

Choose the correct answer.

| ovary | A | | uterus | C |
| oviduct | B | | vagina | D |

(c) What happens during gestation ?

1 mark

_____

(d) Smoking is thought to affect the development of a baby inside its mother.
The diagram shows information about a group of mothers and their babies.

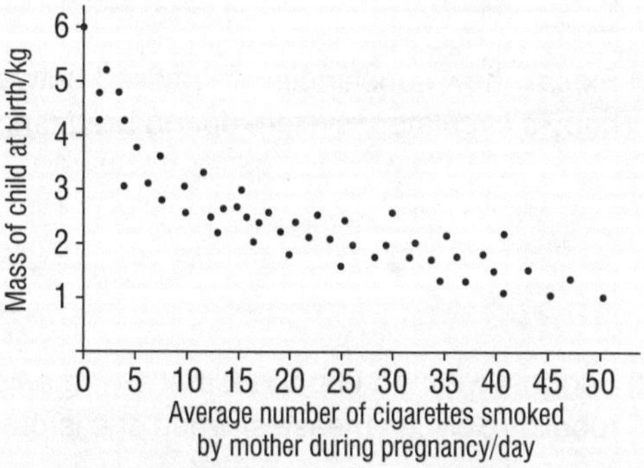

Mass of child at birth/kg

Average number of cigarettes smoked by mother during pregnancy/day

(i) Complete the table below.

2 marks

| highest birth mass | 6 kg | number of cigarettes smoked | |
| lowest birth mass | | number of cigarettes smoked | 50 |

(ii) What is the pattern between a mother smoking during pregnancy and the birth mass of her child ?

1 mark

_____

_____

maximum 6 marks

1. The table shows the average birth masses of babies born to three different groups of mothers.

group	average birth mass in kg
heavy smokers	3.15
light smokers	3.27
non-smokers	3.48

(a) In what way does smoking affect the birth mass of babies ?

1 mark

_____

(b) The mass of babies born to non-smokers is 3.48 kg. It is an average value.
This average value includes babies who weighed less than 3 kg and more than 4 kg.
State **two** reasons why the birth masses of babies born to non-smokers can be so variable.

2 marks

1 _____

2 _____

(c) Explain how substances are passed between a mother's circulatory system and the baby's circulatory system during pregnancy.

1 mark

_____

_____

(d) Suggest why is it important that a woman should not contract certain illnesses such as rubella (German measles) when she is pregnant.

1 mark

_____

_____

(e) What can we do to make sure that teenage girls don't become ill with rubella in later life ?

_____

_____

1 mark

maximum 6 marks

2. The diagram shows a side view of the female reproductive system.

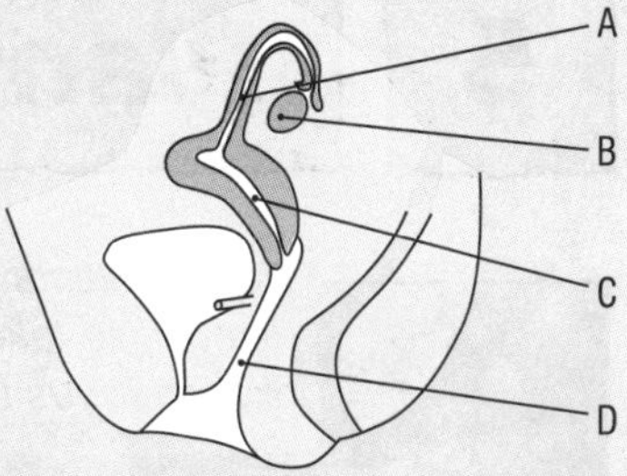

(a) Name the parts labelled A and B.

2 marks

A is _____

B is _____

(b) In which of the parts, A, B, C or D, on the diagram :

2 marks

(i) does fertilisation normally occur ? _____

(ii) does a fertilised egg normally become attached and develop ? _____

(c) During pregnancy a woman must be careful about the things she eats and drinks. Suggest two things she may need to change in her diet for the benefit of her developing child.

2 marks

1 _____

2 _____

(d) The placenta may be described as the 'intestines, lungs and kidneys' of the baby as it develops inside its mother. How does the placenta act as :

3 marks

(i) the intestines ? _____

_____

(ii) the lungs ? _____

_____

(iii) the kidneys ? _____

_____

(e) Adolescence is a time when changes take place to young people.
State one physical change and one emotional change which occurs to young people during adolescence.

2 marks

Physical change _____

Emotional change _____

maximum 11 marks

5 Plants at work

We use plants for food, fuel, building materials and medicines. Plants also take waste carbon dioxide out of the air and make oxygen for us to breathe.

What you need to know

- Green plants use chlorophyll to trap light energy.
- Green plants use this energy to change carbon dioxide and water into sugar and oxygen. This is called photosynthesis.

$$\text{carbon dioxide} + \text{water} \xrightarrow[\text{chlorophyll}]{\text{light energy}} \text{sugar} + \text{oxygen}$$

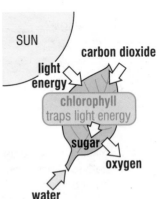

- Plants release oxygen which animals can use for respiration.
- They also use up waste carbon dioxide.
- Plants also use oxygen for their own respiration.

- Plants also need nutrients from the soil, such as nitrates, for healthy growth.
  Fertilisers are used to add extra nutrients to the soil.
  Root hairs absorb water and nutrients from the soil.

- The anthers make pollen grains and the ovary makes ovules.
- Pollination is the transfer of pollen from the anthers to the stigma.
- Fertilisation happens when a pollen nucleus joins with an ovule nucleus.
- After fertilisation, the ovary changes into the fruit and the ovule grows into a seed.
  Under the right conditions the seed can grow into a new plant.

Useful words

carbon dioxide   photosynthesis   chlorophyll

nutrients   oxygen   nitrates   root hairs

respiration   fertilisers   pollination

fertilisation   ovule   fruit   pollen

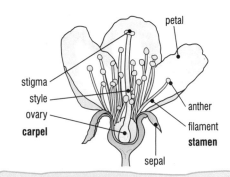

QuickTest..

▶ Green plants have _____ [1] to absorb light energy for

_____ [2] .

Plants use this light energy to make sugar and _____ [3] .

During _____ [4] plants use up _____ [5] and water.

▶ Some of the _____ [6] that plants produce is used by animals for _____ [7] .

Plants also use up some of this _____ [8] for their own _____ [9] .

During _____ [10] plants remove from the air some of the

_____ [11] that is made during _____ [12] .

▶ In addition to _____ [13] and water, plants also need

_____ [14] for healthy growth.

Phosphates and _____ [15] are important plant _____ [16] .

If the soil is lacking in _____ [17] the farmer can add extra ones in the form of

_____ [18] .

Water and _____ [19] are taken up from the soil by _____ [20] .

▶ The anthers make the male cells called _____ [21] grains and the ovary makes the

female cells called _____ [22] .

The transfer of _____ [23] grains from the anthers to the stigma is called _____ [24] .

When the _____ [25] grain nucleus joins with the _____ [26] nucleus, we call it

_____ [27] .

After _____ [28] , the ovary grows into the _____ [29] and the

_____ [30] grows into the seed.

1. (a) The diagram below shows a flowering plant.
Match each of the parts shown to the description of its function.
The first one has been done for you.

3 marks

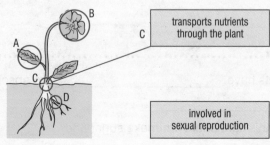

| absorbs water and minerals from the soil | transports nutrients through the plant |
| traps sunlight for photosynthesis | involved in sexual reproduction |

(b) The following gases are present in air.

argon   carbon dioxide   nitrogen   oxygen

Which of these gases is :

2 marks

(i) used up during photosynthesis ? _____

(ii) produced during photosynthesis ? _____

(c) Jill grew some seeds on cotton wool in a dish
near a window. After six days they looked like this :

(i) What substance do we place on the cotton wool
to enable the seeds to germinate and grow ?

1 mark

_____

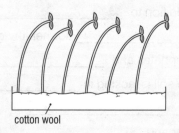

cotton wool

(ii) Explain why the seeds grew like this.

2 marks

_____

_____

(d) Explain why the leaves of a plant are green but the roots are not.

2 marks

_____

_____

maximum 9 marks

2. The drawing shows a flower which has been cut in half. A, B, C and D are parts of the flower.

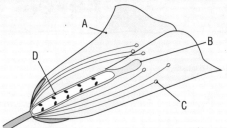

(a) Match each part of the flower to the correct letter.

4 marks

part of flower	letter
anther	
ovary	
petal	
stigma	

(b) Which part of a flower listed in the table above :

4 marks

(i) attracts insects to the flower ? _____

(ii) receives pollen from insects ? _____

(iii) eventually turns into a seed pod ? _____

(iv) makes pollen which rubs off on insects ? _____

(c) The following processes occur during the life cycle of a plant.

        fertilisation   pollination   seed dispersal   seed formation

Write these processes in the correct order in which they occur.

1 mark

        pollination _____ ➩ _____ ➩

_____ ➩ _____

(d) Seeds contain a store of food. Explain why this is needed.

1 mark

_____

_____

maximum 10 marks

33

1. (a) Complete the word equation for photosynthesis.

   1 mark

   _____ + carbon dioxide ⟶ _____ + _____

   (b) Give two reasons why photosynthesis occurs most rapidly
   around the middle of the day.

   2 marks

   1 _____

   2 _____

   (c) Name one element needed for growth by plants which
   they do not get by photosynthesis.
   Explain how this element is obtained.

   2 marks

   Name of element _____

   It is obtained by _____

   _____

   _____

   (d) Complete the following word equation for respiration.

   1 mark

   _____ + _____ ⟶ carbon dioxide + _____

   (e) The diagram shows some parts of a carrot.
   What evidence is there from the structure of the carrot,
   that overall, the rate of photosynthesis
   must be greater than the rate of respiration ?

   1 mark

   _____

   _____

   _____

   _____

   maximum 7 marks

2. The drawing shows a flower that has been cut in half.

(a) During sexual reproduction which parts labelled on the flower will eventually become :

2 marks

(i) a seed ? _____

(ii) a seed pod ? _____

anther

stigma

ovule

ovary

(b) What happens during pollination ?

1 mark

_____

_____

(c) What happens during fertilisation ?

1 mark

_____

_____

(d) *Angraecum sesquipedale* is an orchid from Madagascar.
It has an unusual white flower. The nectary of the flower is at the bottom of a spur 30 cm long.
In 1862 Charles Darwin predicted that this flower was pollinated by a night-flying moth which had a proboscis (mouth-parts) at least 30 cm long.
In 1903 the moth was identified and Darwin was proved correct.

white flower

spur

stem

nectary

Explain how Darwin was able to make his prediction.

3 marks

_____

_____

_____

_____

_____

maximum 7 marks

We inherit many of our features from our parents.
They are passed on from one generation to the next.

What you need to know

- Plants and animals of one kind are called a species.
- There is variation between *different* species eg. differences between dogs and cats.
- There is also variation between individuals of the same species eg. differences between domestic dogs.

- We inherit some features from our parents.
- Other features are caused by our environment.
- Some variation is *gradual* eg. height. Other variation is *clear-cut* eg. eye colour.

- Living things can be put into groups that have similar features.
- Animals with backbones are called vertebrates. Those without backbones are called invertebrates.
- Some plants reproduce by making seeds, others by making spores.

- Useful features can often be bred *into* some animals and plants; less useful features can often be bred *out*.
  Selective breeding can produce new varieties of plants and animals.

Useful words

species   inherit   arthropods

classifying   parents   starfish

environmental   insects

worms   mosses   birds

conifers   fish   molluscs

selective   yield   jellyfish

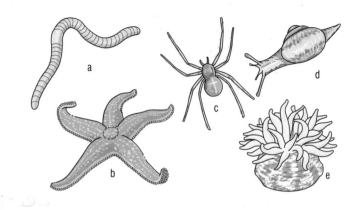

a

b

c

d

e

QuickTest ....

▶ A group of animals or plants that are very similar are of the same _____ [1].

We can divide living things up into groups. The members of these groups have

similar/different [2] features.

▶ We get some of our features from our _____ [3]. We _____ [4] them.

Other features are caused by the way we lead our life. We call them _____ [5].

Put a circle around the features | blood group   speaking French   height   scars
that you think are inherited [6,7,8,9] : | hair length   brown eyes   freckles   neat writing

▶ Putting similar living things into groups is called _____ [10].

Which groups have these features ?

Wings, feathers and can fly : _____ [11]

Long tube-shaped body, made up of segments : _____ [12]

No flowers, seeds are made inside cones : _____ [13]

Live in water, swim using fins and breathe with gills : _____ [14]

6 legs, 3 parts to the body, have wings : _____ [15]

Many have a shell, move on a muscular foot : _____ [16]

Weak roots, thin leaves and make spores : _____ [17]

▶ Humans have used _____ [18] breeding to produce crops with greater _____ [19] and

cattle that make more milk. _____ [20] breeding can eventually lead to new varieties.

▶ Name the animal group to which each of the above animals belongs: a. _____ [21]

b. _____ [22]   c. _____ [23]   d. _____ [24]   e. _____ [25]

37

1. (a) Here are some of the animals that James caught in pitfall traps in his garden.

Snail   Spider   Centipede   Beetle

Match each animal to its description.   *4 marks*

A	Segmented body and many pairs of legs	*Centipede*
B	Segmented body and 6 legs	~~spider beetl~~ *beetle*
C	Soft body covered by a shell	*Snail*
D	Segmented body and 8 legs	*Spider*

(b) James visited the traps in the morning and at night. Here are the results of his investigation for 1 week:

		Snails	Spiders	Centipedes	Beetles		Snails	Spiders	Centipedes	Beetles
Monday	Morning	0	0	0	1	Night	0	2	1	5
Tuesday	Morning	1	0	1	0	Night	0	1	1	1
Wednesday	Morning	0	0	0	0	Night	1	0	2	3
Thursday	Morning	0	1	0	0	Night	1	2	1	2
Friday	Morning	0	0	0	1	Night	1	1	0	1

(i) Which animal is most common in the garden ?

1 mark

Beetle

(ii) When are the animals in the garden most active ?

1 mark

night

(iii) Why was it important for James to visit his traps in the morning and at night ?

1 mark

to give a fair test

(c) One morning James found a strange animal in one of his traps.
This animal belongs to the same group as one of the animals above.
Which one ? Explain why.

2 marks

The same group as the _____ *Spider* _____

because _____ *because it has ~~eigt~~ 8 legs* _____

            maximum 9 marks

2. Here are three different sorts of rabbits. They live in different environments.

Type A   Type B   Type C

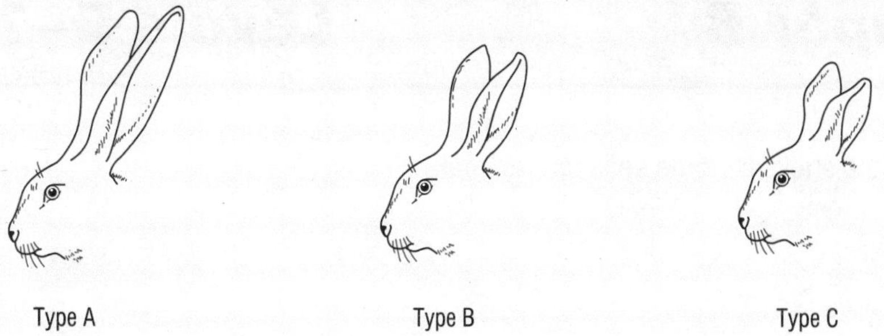

(a) In what way do the rabbits differ in appearance ?

1 mark

_____

(b) (i) Rabbit A lives in hot, open desert. From the information in the diagram explain
        how it is suited to its environment.

1 mark

_____

_____

   (ii) Rabbit C lives in cool, dense forest. From the information in the diagram explain
        how it is suited to its environment.

1 mark

_____

_____

(c) Rabbits A and C will differ in other ways. Give one variation influenced by their
    different environments. Explain your answer.

2 marks

Feature _____

Explanation _____

_____

(d) A breeding colony of type C rabbits was released in the hot open desert. After a
    number of years of breeding, the rabbits were compared with photographs of the
    original colony. How would they be different ?

1 mark

_____

_____

maximum 6 marks

1. The drawings show the shells of some seashore animals.

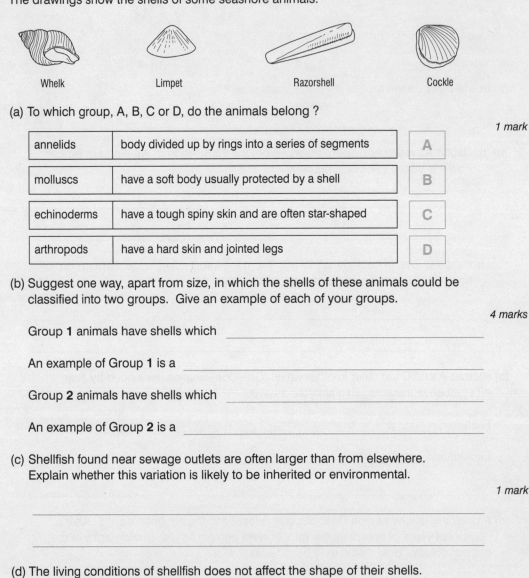

Whelk   Limpet   Razorshell   Cockle

(a) To which group, A, B, C or D, do the animals belong ?

1 mark

annelids	body divided up by rings into a series of segments	A
molluscs	have a soft body usually protected by a shell	B
echinoderms	have a tough spiny skin and are often star-shaped	C
arthropods	have a hard skin and jointed legs	D

(b) Suggest one way, apart from size, in which the shells of these animals could be classified into two groups. Give an example of each of your groups.

4 marks

Group **1** animals have shells which _____

An example of Group **1** is a _____

Group **2** animals have shells which _____

An example of Group **2** is a _____

(c) Shellfish found near sewage outlets are often larger than from elsewhere.
Explain whether this variation is likely to be inherited or environmental.

1 mark

_____

_____

(d) The living conditions of shellfish does not affect the shape of their shells.
What does determine the shape of their shells ?

1 mark

_____

maximum 7 marks

2. Rebecca had to write a description of herself when applying for a summer job.
Here is what she wrote.

I am a girl	I am 1.54 m tall
I weigh 43 kg	I am 17 years old
I have brown hair	I have blue eyes
I speak Welsh	I have pierced ears

(a) From this list choose **two** features which she must have inherited and could not have been affected by her environment.

2 marks

1 _____

2 _____

(b) From this list choose **two** features which may have been inherited but could also have been affected by her environment.

2 marks

1 _____

2 _____

(c) Explain how the environment affects **one** of the features chosen in (b).

1 mark

_____

_____

(d) A graph of the 'weight' of lots of girls of the same age as Rebecca looks like this.

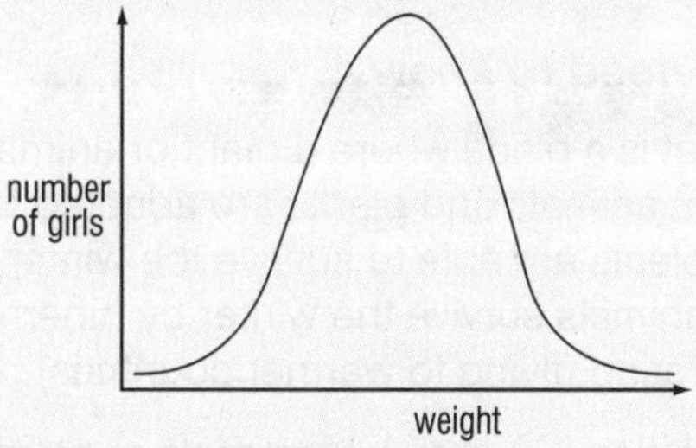

Which **two** of the following would show a similarly shaped distribution ?   *2 marks*

Choose **two** correct boxes.

number of girls

weight

right-handed or left-handed	A	hair colour	C	height	E

length of index finger	B	ability to roll the tongue	D

(e) If a graph of the weights of lots of boys the same age as Rebecca were drawn, how would its shape look compared with the graph above ?

1 mark

_____

maximum 8 marks

Living things depend upon their environment to survive.
They have to compete for things like food and space.
If they are well adapted then their numbers will increase.

What you need to know

- A habitat is a place where a plant or animal lives.
- Different animals and plants are adapted to survive in different habitats.
- Some plants are able to survive the winter as seeds.
- Some animals survive the winter by hibernating (going to sleep) or by migrating (flying to warmer countries).

- A population is a group of animals or plants living in the same habitat.
- Some factors can limit the growth of a population eg. predators, disease and climate.
- Living things compete for resources that are in short supply eg. food and space.
- Living things that compete successfully survive to produce more offspring.
- Predators are adapted to kill other animals (their prey) for food.

- Food chains show what an animal eats and how energy is passed on.
- A food web is made up of many food chains.
- A pyramid of numbers shows the numbers of individuals in a food chain.
- Poisonous chemicals can increase in concentration along food chains.

top carnivore
carnivore
herbivore
producer

Useful words

adaptations   habitat   migrate

seeds   hibernate   population

territory   prey   predators

light   compete   food   limit

space   climate   producers

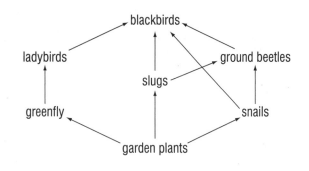

QuickTest ....

▶ The place where a plant or animal lives is its _____ [1].

Living things have special _____ [2] to help them to survive.

Many plants survive the winter as _____ [3]. Some animals _____ [4] (go to sleep for the winter). Some birds _____ [5] (fly to warmer countries).

▶ A _____ [6] is a group of individuals living in the same habitat.

Some factors _____ [7] the growth of a population eg. _____ [8], disease or _____ [9].

Predators are animals that catch and kill their _____ [10] for food.

Living things _____ [11] for resources that are in short supply eg. _____ [12] or space.

Many birds like robins compete for _____ [13].

Weeds compete with other plants for _____ [14], water and _____ [15].

A successful weed produces lots of _____ [16].

▶ In the food web above, garden plants are the _____ [17].

Two predators from the food web are _____ [18] and _____ [19].

If a pollutant killed all the ladybirds then the numbers of greenfly would *rise/fall*[20] and the numbers of blackbirds would *rise/fall*[21].

Complete this food chain : _____ [22] → snails →

_____ _____ [23] → _____ [24].

If a toxic pesticide got into this food chain, which animals would die first ? _____ [25].

▶ Draw a pyramid of numbers for this food chain :

1. Chakeel lives near a desert. He has studied living things in the desert. From his observations he drew a simple food web.

Use only the information in the food web to answer questions (a) and (b).

hawks

snakes   lizards

mice   insects

plants

(a) (i) Write down the **producer** in this food web.

_____

1 mark

(ii) Write down one food chain from this food web. There should be **four** organisms in the food chain.

1 mark

_____ ⟶ _____ ⟶ _____ ⟶ _____

(b) A disease suddenly kills many of the lizards. The disease does not affect the snakes. Complete the sentence below to explain what will happen to the number of snakes.

2 marks

The number of snakes will _____

because _____

_____

(c) Snakes and lizards are most active during the hottest part of the day. At what time would you expect to see most hawks hunting ?

1 mark

Choose the correct box.

2 o'clock during the night   A

8 o'clock in the morning   B

2 o'clock in the afternoon   C

8 o'clock at night   D

maximum 5 marks

2. The diagram below shows parts of three flowers. Insects feed on the nectar at the base of the flower. They draw the nectar up through their proboscis.

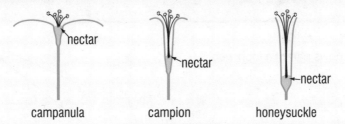

The drawings below show details of three flying insects.

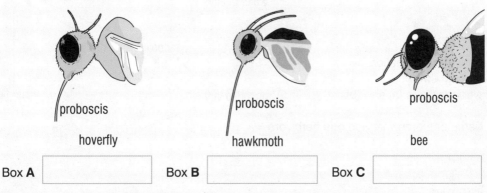

Box **A** [   ]   Box **B** [   ]   Box **C** [   ]

(a) Write the name of the flower each insect is best adapted to feed on.   *3 marks*

(b) (i) Which insect is able to obtain nectar from all of the flowers ?

_____   *1 mark*

   (ii) Which insect is only able to obtain nectar from one of the flowers ?

_____   *1 mark*

(c) All of these insects live and feed in the same environment. Explain why they can all survive together.

_____   *1 mark*

(d) A wasp has a short proboscis. Which of the insects above are most likely to be in competition with wasps ?

_____   *1 mark*

maximum 7 marks

1. The diagram shows part of a food web in a pond.

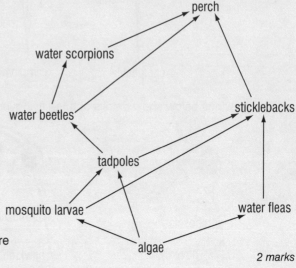

Use only the information in the diagram to answer questions (a) and (b)

(a) Name **one** omnivore and **one** herbivore

2 marks

omnivore _____

herbivore _____

(b) The number of tadpoles in the pond decreases.
    This affects the number of water fleas in the pond.

   (i) Give **one** reason why the number of water fleas might **increase**.

1 mark

   _____

   _____

   (ii) Give **one** reason why the number of water fleas might **decrease**.

1 mark

   _____

   _____

   (iii) Why might the decrease in the number of tadpoles affect the water beetles more than the sticklebacks.

2 marks

   _____

   _____

maximum 6 marks

2. (a) Here are four processes which can change the population of birds in a wood.

> **birth   death   immigration   emigration**

Which **two** of these cause the population of birds in the wood to decrease ?

1 mark

_____

(b) The following table contains information about some woodland birds.

bird	number of eggs laid each year	percentage of adult birds killed each year
chaffinch	10	57
robin	9	50
sparrowhawk	5	33
wood pigeon	6	42

(i) What is the pattern between the number of eggs laid each year and the percentage of adult birds killed ?

1 mark

_____

_____

(ii) About 70 % of adult bluetits die each year. How many eggs are bluetits likely to lay each year ?

1 mark

_____

(c) Bluetits eat insects found on crops in the fields surrounding a wood. Sparrowhawks eat bluetits.

> crops ⇒ insects ⇒ bluetits ⇒ sparrowhawks

Explain how bluetits and sparrowhawks may be poisoned by pesticides sprayed on the crops even though they do not eat the crops.

1 mark

_____

_____

(d) Suggest **one** reason why bluetits find it more difficult to live on open heathland rather than in woodland.

1 mark

_____

maximum 5 marks

8 Matter

Everything around us is solid, liquid or gas.
These 3 states of matter have different properties.
The properties can be explained ...
if you know how the particles in matter are arranged.

Gas particles hit the walls of the balloon.
This causes 'gas pressure'.

What you need to know

| solid | heat → ← cool | liquid | heat → ← cool | gas |

solid	liquid	gas
Particles vibrate about a fixed position	Particles vibrate and change position	Particles move freely in all directions

Properties	Solid	Liquid	Gas
Fixed shape ?	Yes	No – shape of container	No – shape of container
Fixed volume ?	Yes	Yes	No – fills the container
Easily squashed (compressed) ?	Very difficult	Can be compressed	Easy to compress
Flows easily ?	No	Yes	Yes
Dense (heavy for its size) ?	Yes	Less dense than solids	Less dense than liquids

solid ⇌ liquid ⇌ gas

melts / freezes   boils/evaporates / condenses

Density

$$density = \frac{mass}{volume}$$

- Different materials have different melting points, boiling points and densities.

- Most substances expand (get bigger) when they are heated.
  Most substances contract (get smaller) when they are cooled.

- Particles can move and mix themselves. This is diffusion.

- solute + solvent → solution
  (soluble solid)   (liquid)

- The solubility of a solute is different ...
  ... at different temperatures and
  ... in different solvents.

- A saturated solution is made when no more solid can dissolve in the solution at that temperature.

Expanding and contracting

Particles stay the same size ...
they just get
f u r t h e r   a p a r t
or closer together

48

Useful Words

solvent   solute   soluble   insoluble

gases   liquids   solids   diffusion

particles   matter   contraction   saturated

vibrate   melting   freezes   condensation

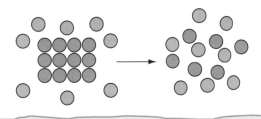

QuickTest..

▶ Gases, _____ [1] and _____ [2] are the 3 states of _____ [3].

  They are made of tiny _____ [4].

▶ When substances are heated the particles _____ [5] more.

  They move further apart. The substance *expands/contracts* [6]. The opposite of expansion is

  _____ [7].

▶ Particles move and mix of their own accord. This is called _____ [8].

  This is why smells spread. _____ [9] diffuse faster than the other 2 states of matter.

▶ A solid changes to a liquid at its _____ [10] point. This is the same temperature as

  when a liquid _____ [11] to form a solid.

  A liquid can change to a gas when heated.

  The liquid *evaporates/condenses* [12]. The opposite of evaporation is _____ [13].

▶ If a substance dissolves, it is _____ [14]. If it does not

  dissolve, it is _____ [15].

  When a _____ [16] dissolves in a _____ [17] it

  forms a solution. If no more more solid can dissolve at that

  temperature, the solution is _____ [18].

  More salt dissolves if the water is *hotter/cooler* [19].

▶ Look at the particle diagram above.

  ● is a sugar particle   ○ is a water particle

  a) What is happening to the sugar cube ? _____ [20]

  b) How could you make the particles move faster ? _____ [21]

49

1. A beaker of water at room temperature was left in a freezer. The graph shows how the temperature in the beaker changes.

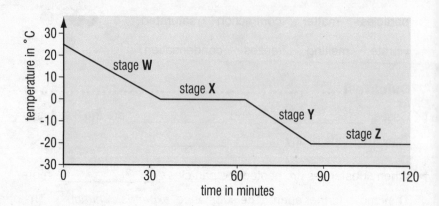

(a) What is happening to the water at stage X ?

1 mark

_____

(b) Why does the temperature stop falling at −20 °C (stage Z) ?

1 mark

_____

(c) Here are four descriptions of the ways in which particles could move.

    A They vibrate about a fixed point

    B They move past each other and are close together

    C They move in straight lines, colliding occasionally

    D They all move at the same speed in the same direction

(i) Which statement best describes how the particles move at stage **W** ? _____ *1 mark*

(ii) Which statement best describes how the particles move at stage **Y** ? _____ *1 mark*

(d) When water is heated it boils and becomes steam. Explain why a small volume of water produces a large amount of steam.

1 mark

_____

_____

maximum 5 marks

2. (a) Complete the following sentence.

When a solid dissolves in a solvent a _____ is formed.   *1 mark*

5.00 g salt

A beaker contains 100.0 g of water.
It is on a balance. The reading on
the balance is 165.0 g. Tom adds
5.0 g of salt. After a short time
all of the salt has dissolved.

water

(b) What is the reading on the balance
after the salt has dissolved ?

_____   *1 mark*

(c) How could the salt be dissolved in the water more quickly ?

1 mark

_____

(d) How could Tom recover all of the salt from the water ?

1 mark

_____

_____

(e) Tom decides to experiment by adding salt to 100 g samples of different solvents until
no more will dissolve.

Which is the most likely outcome of Tom's experiment ?

1 mark

Choose the correct answer.

The same amount of salt will dissolve in 100 g of any solvent.	A
Salt will have different solubilities in different solvents.	B
Salt will dissolve only in water and no other solvents.	C
There is no limit to the amount of salt which can be added to 100 g of a solvent.	D

maximum 5 marks

1. The following table contains information about four chemicals.

chemical	melting point in °C	boiling point in °C	physical state at room temperature, 20°C
butane	−138	−1	gas
glycerol	18	290	
pentane	−130	36	
thymol	52	232	solid

(a) Complete the table by giving the physical state, **solid**, **liquid** or **gas**, of glycerol and pentane at room temperature.

2 marks

Butane gas is used as a fuel for cigarette lighters. It is supplied in cylinders containing liquid butane and butane gas.

(b) Choose **two** correct statements about butane gas in the cylinder.

2 marks

The molecules of gas are :

moving faster than those in the liquid. | A |

moving slower than those in the liquid. | B |

the same distance apart as those in the liquid. | C |

farther apart than those in the liquid. | D |

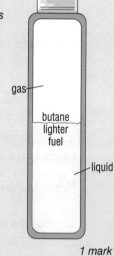

gas

butane
lighter
fuel

liquid

(c) (i) The gas molecules exert a pressure on the walls of the cylinder. How do the gas molecules in the cylinder cause a pressure ?

1 mark

_____

(ii) Explain why the pressure in the cylinder increases when the temperature rises.

2 marks

_____

_____

maximum 7 marks

2. Ammonium chloride dissolves in water to form a solution.

ammonium chloride + water → ammonium chloride solution

(a) Look at equation above: Which substance is the solute and which is the solvent ?

1 mark

Solute = _____ Solvent = _____

(b) What is a saturated solution ?

1 mark

_____

(c) What happens to the particles of ammonium chloride and water as the ammonium chloride dissolves ?

1 mark

_____

(d) Look at the graph: It shows how much ammonium chloride is needed to make 100 g of saturated solution at different temperatures.

Amount of ammonium chloride in 100 g of saturated solution

Temperature/°C

(i) How does the solubility of ammonium chloride change as the temperature rises ?

1 mark

_____

(ii) What mass of ammonium chloride is needed to make 100 g of saturated solution at 50 °C ?

1 mark

_____ g

(iii) At what temperature does 60 g of ammonium chloride dissolve to make 100 g of saturated solution ?

1 mark

_____

(e) Why does the graph only give the solubility of ammonium chloride between 0 °C and 100 °C?

1 mark

_____

maximum 7 marks

9 Elements

Everything around us is made from elements.

What you need to know

- Everything is made from very small particles called atoms. An element contains only one type of atom. Elements are simple substances. They cannot be broken down into anything simpler.

- Each element has a symbol.
  eg. carbon is **C**, magnesium is **Mg**, iron is **Fe**.

- All the elements can be arranged in the Periodic Table.
  The columns of elements in the table are groups.
  The rows are periods.

- All the elements in a group have similar chemical properties.
  They often react in the same way.

- There are 2 main types of element : metals and non-metals.
  Examples of metals are : copper, magnesium, tin and sodium.
  Examples of non-metals are : oxygen, hydrogen, carbon and sulphur.

- Metals are usually hard, shiny solids.
  They often have high melting points.
  They are good conductors of heat and good conductors of electricity.
  A few metals are magnetic eg. iron.

- Non-metals are usually gases or solids with low melting points.
  Most are poor conductors of heat and electricity. They are insulators.
  The solids are often brittle (they break easily).

- Metals are found on the left-hand side of the Periodic Table.
  Non-metals are found on the right-hand side.

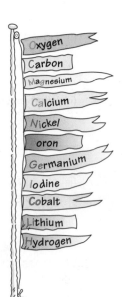

Useful Words

atom symbol

elements conductor

metals non-metals

																	F	
Na	Mg															S	
K																Br	

QuickTest ....

▶ Substances which cannot be broken down into anything

simpler are called _____ [1].

▶ Elements contain only one type of _____ [2]. Each element has its own _____ [3].

▶ There are two main types of elements : _____ [4] and _____ [5].

▶ Copper is a metallic element. It looks *shiny/dull* [6] and is a good

electrical _____ [7].

▶ Element X is hard, shiny and a good thermal conductor. It is not magnetic. It is not brittle.

Is X a metal or a non-metal ? _____ [8]

Which is X most likely to be – sulphur, iron or aluminium ? _____ [9]

▶ Write down the names of the elements with these symbols :

O _____ [10] N _____ [11] C _____ [12] Ca _____ [13]

▶ Look at the outline of the periodic table above. Write down the symbols of :

2 metals in the same group _____ [14] _____ [15]

2 non-metals with similar properties _____ [16] _____ [17]

3 elements in the same period _____ [18] _____ [19] _____ [20]

1 element which is a soft solid – easy to cut with a knife _____ [21]

1 element which is a brown liquid _____ [22]

1 element which is a brittle yellow solid _____ [23]

1 element which is a grey ribbon and burns with a white flame in air _____ [24]

Paper A   Levels 3-6

1. The table below contains information about two elements, X and Y.
   One of these elements is a metal.

	Element X	Element Y
Does it conduct electricity ?	yes	no
Density in g /cm^3	1.70	3.10
Physical state at room temperature	solid	liquid
Chemical reactions	reacts with dilute acid	reacts with element X

(a) Decide which element, X or Y is the metal.

1 mark

The metal is element _____

Using evidence from the table, give two reasons for your answer.

2 marks

1 _____

2 _____

(b) State **one** other property which you would expect the metallic element to have.

1 mark

_____

(c) (i) Which of the following is most likely to be the metal in the table ?

1 mark

Choose the correct answer.

copper   A

magnesium   B

mercury   C

gold   D

(ii) Write the symbol for the metal you have chosen. _____

1 mark

maximum 6 marks

2. The diagram shows part of the Periodic Table.

Li	Be											B	C	N	O	F	Ne
Na	Mg											Al	Si	P	S	Cl	Ar
K	Ca	Sc	Ti	V	Cr	Mn	Fe	Co	Ni	Cu	Zn	Ga	Ge	As	Se	Br	Kr

(a) Copper is a metal and oxygen is a non-metal. Which boxes in the table represent copper and oxygen ?

1 mark

(b) Look at the boxes below. The lines link one property of copper and one property of oxygen to each element.

Match **two** more properties to **each** element.

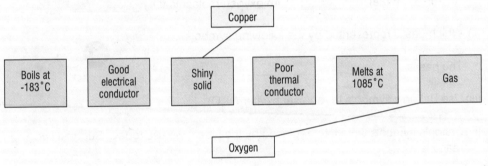

4 marks

(c) Copper is used to make electrical cables. Look at the boxes above and choose two properties of copper which make it suitable for this use.

2 marks

1 _____

2 _____

(d) Iron is also a metal. State one property of iron which copper does not have.

1 mark

_____

(e) Carbon is a non-metal. State one property of carbon which oxygen does not have.

1 mark

_____

maximum 9 marks

1. (a) In the early 19th century the chemist John Dalton listed a series of symbols to represent different elements. Less than 50 elements were known at this time. Some of these symbols are shown below:

carbon   copper   hydrogen   iron   nitrogen   oxygen

A copper atom (Cu) and a nitrogen molecule (N_2) were represented as:

copper atom   nitrogen molecule

(i) Use Dalton's symbols to represent the following:

2 marks

An iron atom (Fe) _____ An oxygen molecule (O_2) _____

(ii) Which gas is represented by the following symbols? *1 mark*

The gas is _____ .

(iii) Use Dalton's symbols to represent water (H_2O) _____ *1 mark*

(iv) Dalton's symbols were later replaced by the letters we use today. Suggest two reasons why.

2 marks

1 _____

2 _____

(b) In the table below which are the properties of a typical non-metal ? *1 mark*

property	good	poor
conductor of electricity		
conductor of heat		

(c) Elements can be arranged in the **Periodic Table**. The diagram shows part of the Periodic Table. Which region of the table contains the non-metals ?

1 mark

maximum 8 marks

2. The table below gives some information about four elements.

element	melting point in °C	boiling point in °C	good electrical conductor	good heat conductor	element is a metal	element is a non-metal
A	1085	2595	yes	yes		
B	−7	59	no	no		
C	−39	357	yes	yes		
D	115	184	no	no		

(a) (i) Decide whether each of the elements is a metal or a non-metal.   *1 mark*

(ii) State **one other** property you would expect element A to have apart from the ones given in the table.

1 mark

_____

(b) What is the physical state of each element at room temperature 20°C – solid, liquid or gas ?

Element A is a _____

Element B is a _____

Element C is a _____

Element D is a _____

1 mark

(c) The properties of metals are similar but not identical. Here is a list of metals.

          copper   iron   lead   mercury   tin   zinc

State one property :

(i) of iron which the other metals in the list do not have ;   *1 mark*

_____

(ii) of mercury which the other metals in the list do not have.   *1 mark*

_____

maximum 5 marks

Water is a compound which keeps us alive.
It is made from hydrogen and oxygen ...
but it's not like either of these elements.

What you need to know ....

- Each element contains only one type of atom.
  Compounds have 2 or more different atoms joined together.

- When atoms join together they make molecules.

  molecules of the element nitrogen, N₂   molecules of the compound water, H₂0

- Elements combine to make compounds. This happens in a chemical reaction.
  We can show a chemical reaction by a word equation.
  eg. magnesium + oxygen → magnesium oxide

- A compound has a fixed composition. Each compound has its own formula.
  eg. magnesium oxide is always MgO.

- A mixture contains more than one substance.
  It does not have fixed composition.
  The parts that make up the mixture are not combined.
  eg. air is a mixture of nitrogen, oxygen, carbon dioxide and other substances.

- Usually we can separate a mixture into pure substances.
  Methods we can use are :
  - filtration   (to separate an insoluble solid from a liquid)
  - distillation   (to separate pure liquids from solutions)
  - chromatography   (to separate mixtures of colours)

Useful Words

pure   mixture

atoms   molecule   reaction

composition   dissolve

evaporate   filter   chromatography

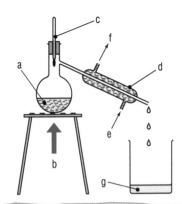

QuickTest...

▶ A compound is made by a chemical _____ [1].

The compound has a fixed _____ [2]. It always has the *same/different*[3] formula.

▶ A _____ [4] of carbon dioxide has the formula CO_2.

1 carbon atom combines with 2 oxygen _____ [5].

▶ A _____ [6] substance contains just one element or one compound.

A _____ [7] contains more than one substance. The substances are *easy/difficult*[8]

to separate.

▶ To separate inks of different colours we use _____ [9].

To separate salt from sand we :

1. add warm water to _____ [10] the salt,

2. _____ [11] the mixture to collect the sand,

3. heat the filtrate to _____ [12] the water from the salt solution.

▶ Distillation (see diagram above) can be used to get pure water from sea water.

Complete the labels for the diagram.

a. _____ [13]   b. _____ [14]

c. _____ [15]   d. _____ [16]   e. _____ [17]

f. _____ [18]   g. _____ [19]

▶ Write E, C, or M to show which of these are **e**lements, **c**ompounds or **m**ixtures.

muddy water ____ [20]   gold ____ [21]   crude oil ____ [22]   hydrogen ____ [23]   copper oxide ____ [24]

water ____ [25]

1. The following diagrams show two methods of separation.

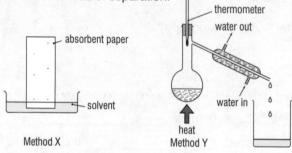

Method X

Method Y

(a) What is the name of each method ?

2 marks

Method X is called _____ .

Method Y is called _____ .

(b) Here are four mixtures. You can separate one mixture by method X, and one mixture by method Y.
Choose X or Y for each box.

2 marks

Box **A** [ ] sand and iron filings   Box **C** [ ] colours in an ink

Box **B** [ ] ethanol and water   Box **D** [ ] salt solution and sand

The diagram below shows the stages in getting pure copper(II) sulphate from copper ore.

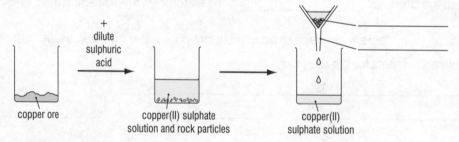

copper ore

+
dilute
sulphuric
acid

copper(II) sulphate
solution and rock particles

copper(II)
sulphate solution

(c) Complete the two labels.

2 marks

(d) How could you get copper(II) sulphate crystals from the solution ?

1 mark

_____

maximum 7 marks

2. Here is a list of common gases. (The formula of each gas is also given to help you.)

chlorine (Cl_2)   hydrogen chloride (HCl)
methane (CH_4)   helium (He)
oxygen (O_2)   sulphur dioxide (SO_2)

(a) Put each gas from the list into the correct column of the table.
You may write the names or the formulae.

2 marks

element	compound

(b) When carbon is burnt in air it reacts with oxygen to form carbon dioxide gas.
Write a word equation to show this reaction.

1 mark

_____

(c) The boxes show some
diagrams of particles.
Match oxygen and carbon
dioxide molecules to their
correct diagrams.
Helium has already been
done for you.

2 marks

Atoms of helium

Molecules of oxygen

Molecules of carbon dioxide

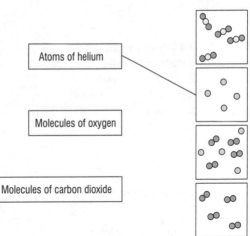

(d) Air contains several gases
including nitrogen, oxygen and carbon dioxide.
Explain why it is a **mixture** and not a compound.

1 mark

_____

_____

(e) When air is cooled it becomes a liquid. The gases in air have different boiling points.
Name a process which could be used to separate the gases in the liquid.

1 mark

_____

maximum 7 marks

1. An unknown pupil has used marker pens to write on the classroom wall. Mr Ward has discovered two pupils with sets of marker pens. He is going to use chromatography to investigate whose pens were used.

   He obtained samples of three coloured inks by wiping the writing on the classroom wall with cotton wool dipped in different solvents. The table shows his observations.

solvent	red ink	green ink	blue ink
water	no effect	no effect	no effect
ethanol	some traces left	removed the ink	some traces left
hexane	removed the ink	removed the ink	removed the ink

(a) Explain which solvent would be most suitable to use for investigating the inks.

1 mark

_____

(b) Mr Ward used this apparatus to separate the dyes in the inks.
Why was the base line drawn in pencil and not ink ? *1 mark*

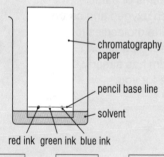

chromatography paper

pencil base line

solvent

red ink green ink blue ink

_____

_____

(c) Here are the results of Mr Ward's investigation.

(i) Which colour ink contained only one dye ? *1 mark*

R   G   B
ink from the classroom wall

R   G   B
ink from pupil X pens

R   G   B
ink from pupil Y pens

_____

(ii) Explain how Mr Ward was able to decide which boy's pens had been used for drawing on the classroom wall.

2 marks

_____

_____

maximum 5 marks

2. (a) Natural gas consists of a mixture of mainly methane (CH_4) together with small amounts of other gases.
Why is natural gas described as a mixture and not a compound ?

1 mark

_____

_____

(b) When methane burns it reacts with oxygen (O_2) in air to form carbon dioxide and water.
Choose answers from the table showing whether the substance is an element or a compound and the number of atoms in one molecule of the substance. The first row has been done for you.

3 marks

substance	it is an element	it is a compound	number of atoms in one molecule
carbon dioxide		✔	3
methane			
oxygen			
water			

(c) The left-hand diagram represents a mixture of methane and oxygen. Draw a similar diagram to represent a mixture of carbon dioxide and water.

1 mark

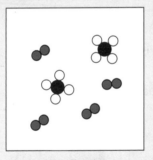

mixture of methane
and oxygen

mixture of carbon dioxide
and water

(d) Describe a chemical test you could do to show that a mixture of carbon dioxide and water has different properties from those of a mixture of methane and oxygen.

1 mark

_____

_____

_____

maximum 6 marks

Chemical reactions

Nearly all the materials around us are made by chemical reactions.
Some chemical reactions are really important...
they are keeping you alive today!

What you need to know..

- Scientists talk about 2 kinds of changes – chemical changes and physical changes.

- In a chemical change one or more new substances are made. But there is
  no change in the total mass before and after the reaction. The same atoms are still there
  but they are combined in different ways.
  Chemical changes are usually difficult to reverse.

- In a physical change no new substances are made. There is no change in mass.
  Physical changes are usually easy to reverse.

- Word equations show us the reactants and products in a reaction.
  eg. magnesium + oxygen → magnesium oxide
         (reactants)   (products)
      iron + chlorine → iron chloride
      iron + sulphur → iron sulphide

- There are different **types** of reaction.
  eg. when something gains oxygen, this is an **oxidation**.

- Some reactions are very useful to us.
  eg. – setting superglue.
      – burning a fuel to keep us warm.

- Some reactions are not useful to us.
  eg. – iron rusting when it reacts with air and water
      – fossil fuels making acid rain when they burn.

- Reactions which take in energy from the surroundings are endothermic.
  Reactions which give out energy are exothermic.

Useful Words

chemical   reactants   product

mass   physical   temperature

combustion   thermal decomposition

neutralisation   reduction

fermentation

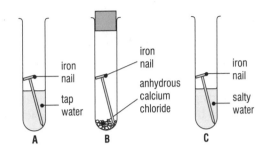

QuickTest ....

▶ Ice melts to form water. This is a _____[1] change. It is *easy/difficult*[2] to get the ice back again.

Baking a cake is a _____[3] change. It is *easy/difficult*[4] to get the ingredients back again.

In physical and chemical changes _____[5] is conserved (stays the same).

▶ Copper reacts with oxygen to make copper oxide.

Copper and oxygen are the _____[6]. Copper oxide is the _____[7].

▶ Burning a fuel is an *exothermic/endothermic*[8] reaction. It gives us energy. This increases the _____[9] of the surroundings.

▶ An acid reacting with a base is called _____[10].

A fuel burning in air is called _____[11].

Taking away the oxygen is called _____[12].

Heating a substance to break it down is called _____[13].

Turning sugar into alcohol is called _____[14].

▶ Complete the word equations :

calcium + oxygen → _____[15]

magnesium + _____[16] → magnesium chloride

iron + sulphur → _____[17]

▶ Look at the test tubes in the diagram. After 5 days which tube would have :

no rusting ___[18] ;   some rusting ___[19] ;   lots of rusting ___[20]

1. (a) The diagrams represent some chemical reactions. Match each diagram to the word which best describes the chemical reaction taking place.

   4 marks

   | Electrolysis | Neutralisation | Rusting | Combustion |

   A   B   C   D

   (b) We place four clean iron nails in sealed tubes containing different things. Then we leave them for one week.

   A ← drying agent   B ← sea water   C ← tap water   D ← boiled water containing no air

   (i) In which **two** of the tubes will the nails **not** rust? _____ and _____

   1 mark

   (ii) In which tube did the nail rust the most? _____

   1 mark

   (c) A clean iron nail had a mass of 11.20 g. It was left to rust for one week. It was found that 0.05 g of oxygen had been used in the reaction.

   What was the mass of the rusty nail? _____

   1 mark

   (d) Iron objects can rust easily, even when we keep them indoors. State two ways in which we can prevent an iron object from rusting.

   2 marks

   1 _____

   2 _____

   maximum 9 marks

2. (a) Which **one** of the following words best describes a combustion reaction ?

1 mark

corrosion　　　A　　　　　　　neutralisation　　　C

decomposition　　　B　　　　　　　oxidation　　　D

Look at the pie charts. They show the relative amounts of four pollutants released as gases from power stations and road traffic.

Power Station

Road Traffic

(b) Which **two** of these pollutants cause acid rain ?

2 marks

1 _____

2 _____

(c) State **two** differences between the mixture of gases from power stations and the mixture of gases from road traffic.

2 marks

1 _____

2 _____

(d) The two products of complete combustion of petrol are not given in the chart. Complete the following word equation for the complete combustion of petrol.

1 mark

petrol + oxygen ⟶ _____ _____ + water

(e) Acid rain causes damage to the environment. Describe one other damaging effect that the pollutants released by power stations and road traffic have on the environment.

1 mark

_____

maximum 7 marks

1. (a) The diagram shows the names of some raw materials and the products made from them. Match each raw material to the correct product. The first one has been done for you.

   3 marks

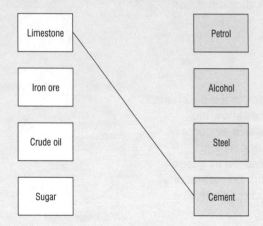

(b) Limestone is mainly calcium carbonate ($CaCO_3$). When we heat it strongly the following reaction takes place.

   calcium carbonate ⟶ calcium oxide + carbon dioxide.

   What type of chemical reaction takes place ? _____   *1 mark*

(c) Calcium oxide is sometimes spread on fields. It increases the pH of soil. What type of substance is calcium oxide ?

   2 marks

   Calcium oxide is a _____ .

   What type of reaction takes place in the soil ?

   A _____ reaction takes place in the soil.

(d) Car engines release pollutant gases into the atmosphere. Explain why limestone buildings in cities often show signs of damage.

   2 marks

   _____

   _____

   _____

   maximum 8 marks

2. In 1774 Joseph Priestley carried out experiments with red mercury oxide and discovered oxygen.

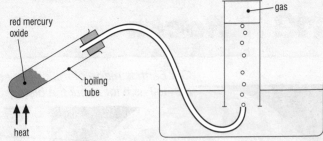

He noticed that when solid red mercury oxide was heated it turned into a grey shiny liquid. Priestley recognised that the liquid was mercury. It also gave off a gas.

(a) (i) State two pieces of evidence that led Priestley to think that a chemical reaction had taken place.

2 marks

1 _____

2 _____

(ii) What further evidence would you expect to get by weighing the boiling tube before and after heating?

1 mark

_____

(b) Write a word equation for this reaction.

1 mark

_____

(c) Name the type of reaction that takes place to form mercury.

1 mark

A _____ reaction takes place.

(d) Priestley tried placing his new gas over a burning candle.

(i) Complete the following sentences.

2 marks

Melting candle wax is an example of a _____ change.

Burning candle wax is an example of a _____ change.

(ii) What type of reaction takes place during the combustion of a fuel?

1 mark

_____

(iii) Priestley found that a candle burned far more brightly in the oxygen than it did in air. Explain why.

1 mark

_____

maximum 9 marks

12 | Rocks

Our Earth is made of rock. The study of rocks can tell us a lot about the history of the Earth.

What you need to know ....

- Most rocks are mixtures. They contain different minerals.

- All rocks slowly crumble away. They are weakened by the weather. This process is called weathering. Weathering can be caused by water, wind and changes in temperature. Rocks expand as they get hotter and contract when they get cooler.

- The small pieces of rock rub against each other as they are moved, eg. by wind and rivers. They wear away. This process is called erosion. The rock pieces can be transported and deposited in another place.

- There are 3 main types of rock – igneous, sedimentary and metamorphic. The 3 types form in different ways.

- Igneous rocks form when melted (molten) substances cool. They are hard and made of crystals. Larger crystals form when the cooling is slow. Granite is an igneous rock.

- Sedimentary rocks form in layers. They are made when substances settle out in water. In hot weather, water from seas and lakes can run dry. A sediment can form. Sometimes these rocks contain fossils. The rocks are usually soft. Sandstone is a sedimentary rock.

- Metamorphic rocks are made when rocks are heated and/or squashed together. They form very slowly. They are usually very hard. Marble is a metamorphic rock.

- Over millions of years one rock type can change into another. The rocks are recycled. We call this the rock cycle. (See the diagram at the top of page 73.)

Useful Words

contract   expand

igneous   sedimentary

metamorphic

weathering

freezes   acid rain

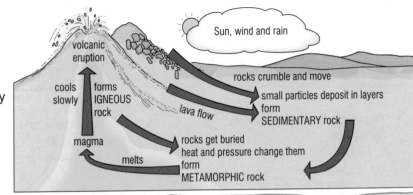

Sun, wind and rain

volcanic eruption

rocks crumble and move

cools slowly   forms IGNEOUS rock

lava flow

small particles deposit in layers form SEDIMENTARY rock

magma

melts

rocks get buried heat and pressure change them form METAMORPHIC rock

QuickTest..

▶ Rocks _____ [1] as they get hotter. They _____ [2] as they cool.

Expansion and contraction can shatter a rock.

This is called _____ [3]. Rocks can also crumble when water

_____ [4] in their cracks. Some rocks are broken down by chemical weathering

eg. limestone is dissolved away by _____ [5].

▶ Basalt is an _____ [6] rock. It contains *small/large* [7] crystals because it is formed

from lava which cools quickly on the Earth's surface. Granite contains *smaller/larger* [8]

crystals. It forms from the slow cooling of magma.

▶ Chalk forms from layers of tiny shellfish compressed together.

It is a _____ [9] rock.

▶ Chalk can be changed to marble by heat and pressure.

Marble is a _____ [10] rock.

weathering

_____ [14]

_____ [11]

_____ [13]

_____ [12]

Put the labels below in the right order for the cycle.

– rocks transported

– new rocks formed

– erosion

– rocks deposited

1. The diagram shows a simple rock cycle.

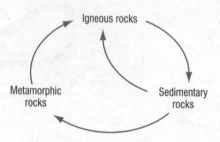

(a) (i) Sedimentary rocks may change into metamorphic rocks. State **two** causes of this change   *2 marks*

1 _____   2 _____

(ii) Marble is a metamorphic rock. From which sedimentary rock listed below is it formed ?

1 mark

sandstone   A   mudstone   B   limestone   C   siltstone   D

(b) Sedimentary rocks and metamorphic rocks may change into igneous rocks. Which **one** of the following is an igneous rock ?

1 mark

sandstone   A   basalt   B   slate   C   chalk   D

(c) Igneous rocks may be changed back into sedimentary rocks. This involves several processes.
On the diagram write the letter X, Y, or Z to show :   (i)   where deposition occurs   **X**

(ii)   where weathering occurs   **Y**

(iii)   where transport occurs.   **Z**

3 marks

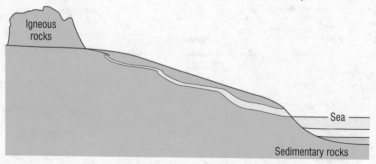

maximum 7 marks

2. The diagram shows the structure of some rocks beneath the ground.

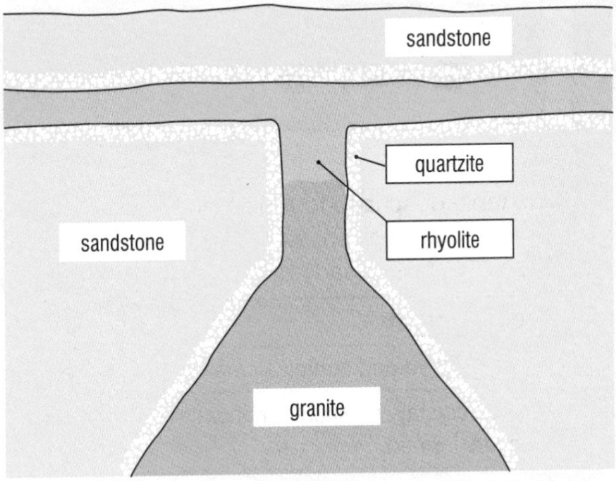

(a) Which **two** of the rocks in the diagram formed from magma that had cooled ? *1 mark*

granite [A]   rhyolite [C]

quartzite [B]   sandstone [D]

(b) Explain why the sandstone has turned to the metamorphic rock quartzite around the igneous rocks.

1 mark

_____

_____

(c) (i) Which is the oldest rock shown in the structure ? _____ *1 mark*

(ii) State **one** piece of evidence from the diagram which indicates this.

1 mark

_____

_____

(d) The diagram shows the crystals in granite and rhyolite.

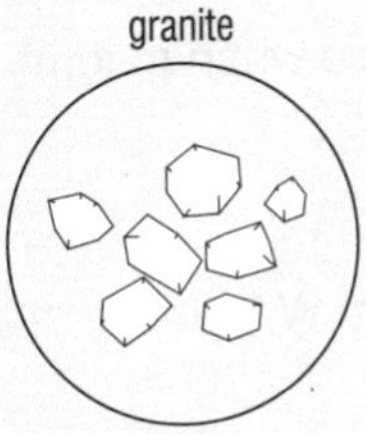

Why are the crystals in granite larger than those in rhyolite ?

1 mark

_____

maximum 5 marks

1. The following table describes four different rocks, A, B, C and D.

   (a) From the information given, state whether each rock is sedimentary, igneous or metamorphic. A has already been done for you.

   3 marks

rock	description	type of rock
A	fine grained and contains small pieces of shell	sedimentary
B	large crystals of different minerals in no regular pattern; no layers formed	
C	crystalline, containing bands of different minerals	
D	composed of small rounded grains of sand of similar size	

   In the rock structure shown magma has forced its way through a sedimentary rock forming an igneous intrusion.

   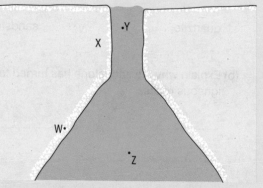

   (b) Which of the rocks in the table could be found at :

   2 marks

   (i) point W ? _____

   (ii) point Z ? _____

   (c) Explain why the crystal size in the rocks at Y and Z is different.

   2 marks

   _____

   _____

   _____

   (d) What change of state takes place when magma crystallises to form igneous rock ?

   1 mark

   From _____ to _____ .

   (e) Explain why the band of rocks at W is thicker than the band of rocks at X.

   1 mark

   _____

   _____

maximum 9 marks

2. (a) How long does it take for most sedimentary rocks to form ?

1 mark

Choose the correct answer.

tens of years   A   thousands of years   C

hundreds of years   B   millions of years   D

(b) In the desert the days are very hot and the nights are very cold.
Explain how this causes rocks to weather.

2 marks

_____

_____

(c) The diagram on the right shows
details of the surface of sandstone.

This sandstone is in an area which
has wet and very cold winters.
Explain how these conditions cause
the sandstone to weather.

2 marks

Sandstone

_____

_____

(d) The maximum size of grains of
sand which can be carried in water
depends on the speed of the water
current.

Use the information in the diagram
to explain how a sediment might
form at the mouth of a river.

2 marks

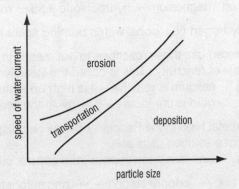

speed of water current

erosion

transportation

deposition

particle size

_____

_____

_____

maximum 7 marks

Some metals are more reactive than others.
We can put them in order of reactivity.

What you need to know

- Metals can react with :
  - oxygen to make oxides eg. copper + oxygen → copper oxide
  - water to make hydrogen gas
    eg. sodium + water → sodium hydroxide + hydrogen
  - acid to make hydrogen gas
    eg. magnesium + hydrochloric acid → magnesium chloride + hydrogen

  (Hydrogen gas 'pops' with a burning splint.)

- We can use these reactions to put metals in a league
  table of reactivity. This is called the Reactivity Series.
  eg.   calcium is reactive – it is high up in the series
        gold is unreactive – it is low in the series.

- A metal high in the Reactivity Series can displace one lower,
  from a solution of its salt.
  eg.   zinc displaces copper from copper sulphate solution

     zinc + copper sulphate → zinc sulphate + copper
  (silver grey)(blue solution) (colourless solution)(pink brown)

- The Reactivity Series can be used to make predictions about reactions.
  Q. magnesium + copper oxide → ?
  A. magnesium is more reactive than copper – so it displaces copper.

  magnesium + copper oxide → magnesium oxide + copper
  (silver-grey)   (black)   (grey-white)   (brown)

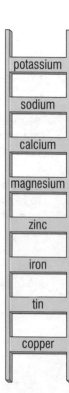

potassium

sodium

calcium

magnesium

zinc

iron

tin

copper

Useful Words

Reactivity Series   reactive

metals   displaces

hydrogen

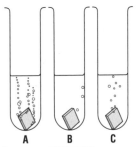

A   B   C

QuickTest..

▶ The league table for _____ [1] is called the

_____ [2] .

▶ Sodium is a _____ [3] metal. It reacts quickly with water to make _____ [4] gas.

▶ Zinc is more reactive than tin. It _____ [5] tin from tin chloride solution.

▶ Complete the word equations :

magnesium + water (steam) → magnesium oxide + _____ [6]

iron + hydrochloric acid → iron chloride + _____ [7]

calcium + oxygen → _____ [8]

▶ Use the Reactivity Series to finish the word equations :

magnesium + copper sulphate → _____ + _____ [9, 10]

tin + zinc chloride → _____ + _____ [11, 12]

zinc + copper oxide → _____ + _____ [13, 14]

▶ Metal X reacts quickly with cold water.

Metal Y does not react with cold water or steam.

Metal Z reacts slowly with cold water and quickly with steam.

Put X, Y and Z in order of reactivity   ___ [15] (most reactive);   ___ [16] ;   ___ [17] (least reactive)

▶ The diagram above shows 3 metals in acid.

Put the metals in order of reactivity. Explain your answer.

___ [18] (most reactive);   ___ [19] ;   ___ [20] (least reactive)

Explanation _____

_____ [21]

1. The two diagrams below show the reaction of four metals with cold water and with dilute nitric acid.

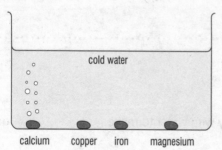

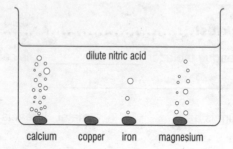

Use the information above to answer the following questions.

(a) Name a metal which reacts with cold water. _____

1 mark

(b) Name a metal which reacts with dilute nitric acid but not with cold water.

1 mark

_____

(c) Which metal does not react with cold water or dilute nitric acid ?

1 mark

_____

(d) Arrange the metals in order of reactivity with the **most** reactive at the top. *1 mark*

_____   **most reactive**

_____

_____

_____   **least reactive**

(e) Complete the following word equation for the reaction of calcium with dilute nitric acid.

1 mark

calcium + dilute nitric acid ➝ calcium nitrate + _____

maximum 5 marks

2. Laura carried out some experiments to investigate the reactivity of four metals.
Here are her results.

Metal	copper sulphate solution	iron sulphate solution	magnesium sulphate solution	zinc sulphate solution
copper		✗	✗	✗
iron	✔		✗	✗
magnesium	✔	✔		✔
zinc	✔	✔	✗	

(a) From Laura's results write down the order of reactivity of these metals.

1 mark

_____ **most reactive**

_____

_____ ↑

_____ **least reactive**

(b) Complete this word equation.

1 mark

zinc + copper sulphate ⟶ _____ + _____

(c) Copper metal is brown and copper sulphate solution is blue.
Write down **two** things which Laura would see when she reacted zinc with copper sulphate solution.

2 marks

1 _____

2 _____

(d) (i) One of the metals in the table reacts with warm water giving hydrogen.
Which metal is this most likely to be ?

1 mark

_____

(ii) Which metal would be best to make pipes which carry warm water ?

1 mark

_____

maximum 6 marks

Paper B   Levels 5–7

1. The table below contains information about four metals.

metal	reacts readily with		
	cold water	hot water	dilute acid
A	yes	yes	yes
B	no	no	yes
C	no	yes	yes
D	no	no	no

(a) Using the information given in the table, arrange the metals in order of reactivity starting with the **least** reactive.

1 mark

least reactive	➤		most reactive

(b) Using your knowledge of the reactivity of metals suggest which of the metals, A, B, C or D might be :

2 marks

(i) sodium _____   (ii) copper _____

(c) Metal B could be zinc or iron. Zinc is more reactive than iron.
Write a word equation for the reaction between zinc and iron sulphate.

1 mark

_____➤_____

(d) Calcium reacts with cold water.

calcium + water ➤ calcium hydroxide + hydrogen

What does this tell you about the reactivity of calcium compared with the reactivity of hydrogen ?

1 mark

_____

(e) Explain why water should not be used to extinguish a fire involving calcium.

2 marks

_____

_____

maximum 7 marks

2. Here is a reactivity series of elements starting with the most reactive :

sodium   calcium   magnesium   aluminium   carbon   zinc   iron   tin   lead
(most reactive   least reactive)

(a) Some metals can be obtained from their ores by heating with carbon.
Which of these metals can be obtained in this way ?

1 mark

_____

(b) The steel hulls of ships are
protected from rusting by
attaching blocks of other
more reactive metals. The
more reactive metal slowly
corrodes instead of the
steel hull.

steel hull

block of metal

    (i) Give **one** metal from
the list above which
would be suitable for
this purpose.   *1 mark*

_____

    (ii) Give **one** metal from the list above which would be unsuitable for this purpose and
explain why it would be unsuitable.

2 marks

Name of metal   _____

It is unsuitable because   _____

_____

(c) Stewed rhubarb is acidic. It has a pH of about 3.0.

    (i) Suggest why aluminium pans should not be used to cook rhubarb.

1 mark

_____

    (ii) Rhubarb can be cooked in copper pans.
What does this tell you about the reactivity of copper ?

1 mark

_____

maximum 6 marks

14 Acids and alkalis

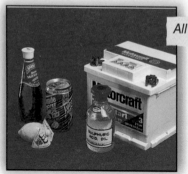

All these contain acids.

All these contain alkalis.

What you need to know

- Acids and alkalis are chemical opposites.
  Alkalis are bases (metal oxides, hydroxides or carbonates) which dissolve in water.

- We can use indicators to show which things are acids and which things are alkalis.
  Coloured berries, flower petals and vegetables make good indicators.

- Universal indicator is a mixture of indicators.
  Its colour gives you the pH number of the substance.

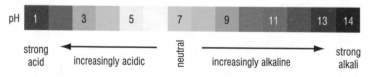

| pH | 1 | 3 | 5 | 7 | 9 | 11 | 13 | 14 |

strong acid ← increasingly acidic | neutral | increasingly alkaline → strong alkali

- Acids can be changed into salts by chemical reactions.
  acid + metal → salt + hydrogen

  acid + base (alkali) → salt + water
  eg. acid + metal oxide → salt + water
  eg. acid + metal carbonate → salt + water + carbon dioxide
     (carbon dioxide gas turns limewater cloudy)

- The acid + base reaction is called neutralisation.
  eg. sulphuric acid + potassium hydroxide → potassium sulphate + water
        (acid)   (base)   (salt)

  Neutralisations are useful reactions.
  eg. Acids damage teeth. Toothpastes contain alkali to neutralise acids in the mouth.
  Some plants grow better in alkaline soil. Lime can be added to change the pH of soil.

- Acids in the atmosphere can cause damage. Acid rain can corrode metal.
  It can dissolve rock (eg. limestone).

Useful Words

pH   acid   alkali

bases   neutralisation

salts   chloride   nitrate

universal indicator

acidic   alkaline

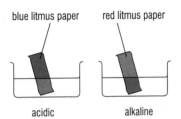

blue litmus paper   red litmus paper

acidic   alkaline

Litmus is a useful indicator. It can be used as paper or liquid.

QuickTest ....

▶ A solution with _____¹ number 7 is neutral.

_____² is green when added to the solution.

▶ The oxides, hydroxides and carbonates of metals are called _____³.

They all react with acids to make _____⁴ + water.

▶ Sulphuric acid is used to make a sulphate. Hydrochloric acid is used to make a

_____⁵. Nitric acid is used to make a _____⁶.

▶ Ammonium sulphate, a fertiliser, can be made from ammonium hydroxide and

sulphuric _____⁷. This is a _____⁸ reaction.

Too much acid in the stomach can cause indigestion. Indigestion tablets contain an

_____⁹ to neutralise this.

▶

Solution	A	B	C	D	E	F
pH Value	9	2	7	10	11	13

What colour does pH paper turn with F ? _____¹⁰

Which solution when mixed with D could form a neutral solution ? ____¹¹

Which solution is the weakest alkali ? ____¹²   Which solution could be water ? ____¹³

Magnesium metal is added to B. What would you expect to see ? _____¹⁴

Sodium carbonate is added to B. What would you expect to see ? _____¹⁵

▶ Complete the word equations :

sodium hydroxide + sulphuric acid → _____¹⁶ + _____¹⁷

copper carbonate + hydrochloric acid →

_____¹⁸ + _____¹⁹ + _____²⁰

85

1. (a) Which **two** of the following statements about acids are true ?

2 marks

Acids turn litmus paper from red to blue	A	Acids are always poisonous	D
Acids react with carbonates	B	Acids damage teeth	E
Acids always dissolve plastics	C	Acids cannot be stored in glass bottles	F

(b) pH paper is used to test whether a solution is acidic, neutral or alkaline.

colour of pH paper	red	orange	yellow	green	blue	purple
pH of solution	0-4	5	6	7	8-10	11-14

(i) Match the property to the substance. The first one has been done for you.   *4 marks*

substance	colour of pH paper	acidic	neutral	alkaline
lemon juice	red	✔		
toothpaste	blue			
distilled water	green			
oven cleaner	purple			
milk	yellow			

(ii) Equal amounts of lemon juice and milk are mixed.
What is the most likely pH of this mixture ?

1 mark

pH 4	A	pH 8	C
pH 7	B	pH 12	D

(c) You add some powdered limestone to lemon juice.
What would you **see** happening ?

1 mark

_____

maximum 8 marks

2. Magnesium reacts with dilute hydrochloric acid, giving off a gas.

(a) Which **one** of the following gases is given off in this reaction ?

1 mark

carbon dioxide	A
chlorine	B
hydrogen	C
oxygen	D

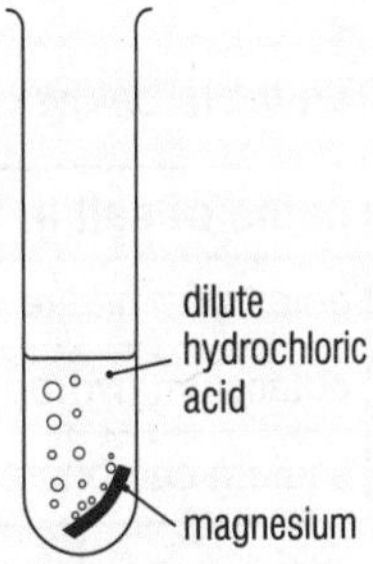

dilute hydrochloric acid

magnesium

(b) Which **one** of the following tests could be used to identify this gas ?

1 mark

Limewater turns milky.	A
A glowing splint relights.	B
A burning splint is put out.	C
A lighted splint pops.	D

(c) What is the name of the salt also produced when magnesium reacts with hydrochloric acid ?

1 mark

_____

(d) At the end of the reaction some magnesium is left unreacted.
How can we get crystals of the salt ?

2 marks

_____

_____

_____

(e) We can make magnesium sulphate in a reaction between magnesium and another acid. Name this other acid.

1 mark

_____

maximum 6 marks

1. The table below gives information about solutions of three different salts in water.

name of salt in the solution	pH of the solution
potassium nitrate	7
potassium hydrogensulphate	3
sodium carbonate	12

(a) Which two of these solutions could form a neutral solution when mixed ?

1 mark

_____ and _____

(b) Sodium carbonate reacts with dilute hydrochloric acid.
   (i) Which gas is produced by this reaction ?

1 mark

_____

   (ii) Describe and give the result of a simple chemical test for this gas.

2 marks

_____

_____

   (iii) What is the name of the salt which is also produced by this reaction ?

1 mark

_____

(c) Limescale is caused by the build up of calcium carbonate.
   Which **one** of the following solutions could be used to remove limescale ?

1 mark

sodium hydroxide   A

universal indicator   B

citric acid   C

sodium chloride   D

maximum 6 marks

2. Soda tablets are used to make water fizzy.
Soda tablets contain sodium hydrogencarbonate.
Here are some properties of sodium hydrogencarbonate :

It is a white solid.

It is not poisonous.

It is soluble in water.

It forms a solution with a pH of about 8.5.

It has no taste.

(a) Is sodium hydrogencarbonate solution acidic, neutral or alkaline ?

1 mark

_____

(b) State **two** pieces of information which tell you that you can drink water containing sodium hydrogencarbonate.

2 marks

1 _____

2 _____

(c) Soda tablets also contain tartaric acid.
This acid reacts with sodium
hydrogencarbonate to form a salt.
This salt is a tartrate.
The reaction is shown
in the word equation below.

sodium hydrogencarbonate + tartaric acid ➡ **x** + carbon dioxide + water

1 mark

What is the name of the product **x** ? _____ .

(d) When a soda tablet is dropped in water a gas is given off which makes the water fizzy.

1 mark

Name this gas. _____

(e) Why must the soda tablets be kept in an airtight bottle ?

1 mark

_____

_____

maximum 6 marks

Energy

Without energy nothing can ever happen !
We get energy from a variety of resources...
but some of these resources are running out.

What you need to know

- To get a job done, energy must be transferred from one place to another.
  Energy can be transferred by electricity, by sound, by light, or by thermal (heat) transfer.
- Heat energy can be transferred by conduction, convection and radiation.

- Energy can exist in several different forms, including : thermal energy (heat), light, sound, electricity, nuclear, chemical energy, etc. 1 kilojoule = 1000 joules.
  Stored energy is called potential energy. Movement energy is called kinetic energy.

- Fuels store energy. Coal, oil and natural gas are fossil fuels. These are non-renewable sources of energy (they get used up). Uranium is another non-renewable source.

- We can also get energy from wind, waves, sunlight (solar energy), hydro-electric dams, tides, geothermal stations, and from biomass (eg. plants). These sources are renewable.

- Electricity can be generated (made) from non-renewable and from renewable resources.
- Most of our energy comes (indirectly) from the Sun.

- The laws of energy :
  1. The amount of energy before a transfer is always equal to the amount of energy after the transfer. We say the energy is 'conserved'.
  2. In energy transfers, the energy spreads out and becomes less useful to us.

- If the temperature of an object rises, its atoms vibrate more.
  The thermal energy (or heat) is the total energy of all the vibrating atoms in the object.

Useful Words

conduction   convection   conserved

kinetic   potential   non-renewable

•transferred   Sun   light   chemical

atoms   thermal   renewable   electricity

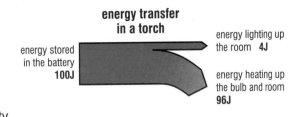

energy transfer in a torch

energy stored in the battery **100J**

energy lighting up the room **4J**

energy heating up the bulb and room **96J**

QuickTest ....

▶ The energy of a moving car is called _____ [1] energy.

The energy of a stone at the top of a cliff is called _____ [2] (stored) energy.

▶ The main fossil fuels are _____ [3], _____ [4], and natural gas. These are

_____ [5] resources.

The energy in coal and oil and natural gas came originally from the _____ [6].

▶ The energy from a hydroelectric dam is a _____ [7] resource.

Name seven renewable sources of energy. _____

_____ [8].

▶ To heat a pan of water, it must be given _____ [9] energy.

If the temperature of a pan rises, its _____ [10] vibrate *more/less* [11].

The total _____ [12] of all the vibrating atoms is called the _____ [13] energy.

The energy is transferred through the pan by _____ [14] and

through the water mainly by _____ [15].

▶ When a clockwork toy is moving, stored (potential) energy in the wound up spring is

_____ [16] to _____ [17] energy.

▶ In a torch (see the diagram), the _____ [18] energy in the battery is transferred by

_____ [19] to the bulb, where it appears as _____ [20] energy and

_____ [21] energy. In this transfer, the total amount of energy is constant (it is

_____ [22]), but afterwards it is spread out and *more/less* [23] useful to us.

91

1. Alex has an electric toy car. The diagram shows the electrical circuit in the car.

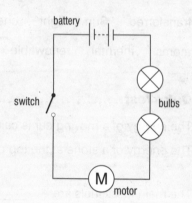

(a) Which part of the circuit is the energy source ?

1 mark

_____

(b) Which term completes this sentence :
Energy is stored in the energy source as …

1 mark

chemical energy	A
kinetic energy	B
light energy	C
thermal energy	D

When the switch is closed the car lights come on and the car moves forward.

(c) The list below gives some different forms of energy.
Use them to answer (c) parts (i) and (ii).

chemical   **electrical**   **heat**   **kinetic**

light   **potential**   **sound**

(i) What **useful** energy transfer takes place in the motor ?

2 marks

_____ energy ⫶➡ _____ energy

(ii) Wasted energy from the bulbs is transferred to the surroundings as

1 mark

_____ energy.

maximum 5 marks

2. (a) Coal is a non-renewable energy source.

   (i) Choose **two** other non-renewable sources.

   2 marks

   wind | A | oil | D |

   fuel crops (biomass) | B | waves | E |

   tidal | C | natural gas | F |

   (ii) Explain why coal is described as a **non-renewable** energy source.

   1 mark

   _____

   _____

(b) Coal is a store of energy. Where did this energy originally come from ?

   1 mark

   _____

(c) Each of the devices shown uses a **different** fuel.
    Match each device to the fuel it uses.
    You must use each fuel only once.

   3 marks

   Petrol

   Gas

(d) The fuels in (c) are described below.
    Name each fuel.   *3 marks*

   Wood

   (i) Fuel A is usually stored under pressure in tanks or small cylinders.

   Fuel A is _____

   (ii) Fuel B is a renewable source of energy.

   Fuel B is _____

   (iii) Fuel C can be stored in tanks not under pressure.

   Fuel C is _____

   maximum 10 marks

1. (a) The table below shows the origins of some energy sources.
   For each source, select **one** answer from the correct column.

4 marks

energy source	obtained directly from the sun	obtained indirectly from the sun	not obtained from the sun
biomass			
geothermal			
solar			
wind			

(b) (i) The diagram below shows the energy transfers which take place
   when petrol burns in a car engine.
   Complete the diagram by filling in the two blank spaces.

2 marks

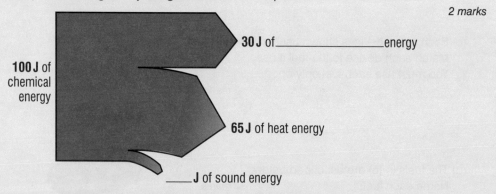

100 J of chemical energy

30 J of_____energy

65 J of heat energy

_____ J of sound energy

(ii) When 1 g of petrol is burned, it gives out 40 kJ of energy.
   How much **useful** energy is provided when 1 g of petrol burns in a car engine ?

1 mark

_____

_____

(c) Energy which does not do useful work is sometimes described as 'lost energy'.
   Is the energy really lost ? Explain your answer.

1 mark

_____

_____

maximum 8 marks

2. In a power station, water is converted to steam. The steam turns a generator, which produces electricity.

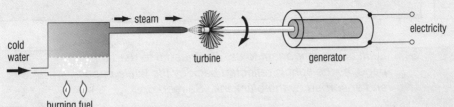

(a) Name **one** energy transfer which takes place in the power station.

1 mark

_____

(b) Not all of the energy released by the fuel is absorbed by the water.
What happens to this 'wasted' energy ?

1 mark

_____

_____

(c) Explain why the 'wasted' energy cannot be used to make steam.

1 mark

_____

_____

(d) Choose words from this list to describe what happens to the water while it is being heated.

decreases   increases   move slower   move faster

3 marks

	during heating
temperature of water :	
motion of water molecules :	
total energy of water :	

(e) Explain what is meant by the **total energy** contained in the water.

1 mark

_____

_____

maximum 7 marks

Light is very important to us. You need it to read this page, as the light is reflected back by the white paper and absorbed by the black ink. So read on . . .

What you need to know

- In air, light travels in a straight line, at a very high speed. In glass it travels more slowly.
- Light travels much faster than sound.
- If light rays are stopped by an object, then a shadow is formed.

- You can see this page because some light rays (from a window or a lamp) are scattered by the paper, and then travel to your eye.

- The law of reflection : the angle of incidence (i) always equals the angle of reflection (r).
- The image in a plane mirror is as far behind the mirror as the object is in front.

- Refraction : when a light ray goes into glass it is refracted (bent) *towards* the normal line. This is because the light slows down in the glass. When light comes out of glass, it is refracted *away from* the normal line.

- When white light goes into a prism (see page 97), it is dispersed into the 7 colours of the spectrum.

- A red filter will let through only red light (which we see). It absorbs all the other colours.
- A green object reflects green light (which we see). It absorbs all the other colours.

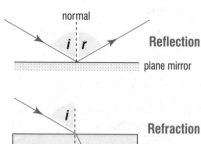

Reflection

Refraction

Useful Words

ray   reflection   incidence

speed   refracted   refraction

absorbs   dispersion   spectrum

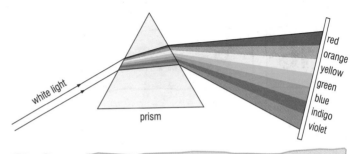

white light

prism

red
orange
yellow
green
blue
indigo
violet

QuickTest ....

▶ Light travels much *slower/faster*[1] than sound.

The law of _____[2] states :

the angle of _____[3] (i) is always equal to the angle of _____[4] (r).

An object is 50 cm in front of a mirror. Where exactly does its image appear to be ?

_____[5]

▶ In air, a light _____[6] travels in a straight line at high _____[7].

If the ray enters a glass block it *slows down/speeds up*[8], and the ray is _____[9]

(bent). In this case it is bent *towards/away from*[10] the normal line.

This is called _____[11].

When a light ray leaves the glass block it is refracted *towards/away from*[12] the normal.

▶ A _____[13] can be used to disperse white light into the 7 colours of the

_____[14]. This is called _____[15].

The 7 colours (in order) are : red, _____[16], _____[17], _____[18],

_____[19], _____[20], _____[21].

▶ A blue filter lets through only _____[22] light. It _____[23] all the other colours.

A red book reflects _____[24] light. It _____[25] all the other colours.

When only blue light shines on a red book, it looks *red/blue/black*[26].

▶ If you hold your hand near a lamp, it makes a shadow on the wall.

Explain why : _____

_____[27]

1. (a) Which **one** of the following statements about light is true ?

1 mark

Light travels more slowly than sound.   A

Light travels at the same speed as sound.   B

Light travels a little more quickly than sound.   C

Light travels much more quickly than sound.   D ✓

(b) The diagram shows a bird's eye view of four children standing around a garden shed.

Amy can see Ben and Danny, but not Claire.
Which pairs of children can see each other ?

4 marks

	Amy	Ben	Claire	Danny
Amy				
Ben				
Claire				
Danny				

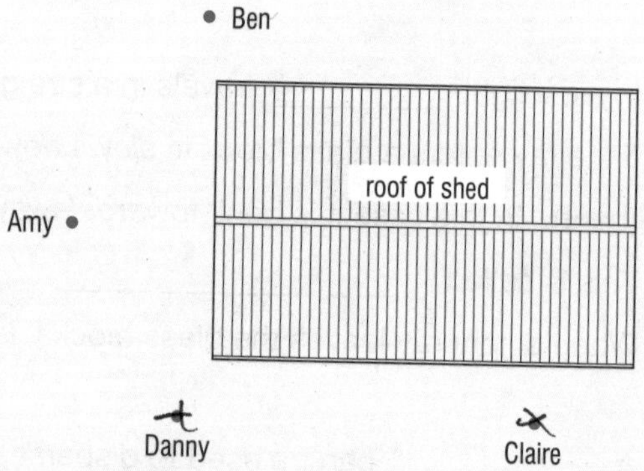

• Ben

Amy •

roof of shed

Danny

Claire

(c) (i) What simple object could Danny hold which would allow Amy to see Claire ?

1 mark

mirro

(ii) How would this object allow Amy to see Claire ?

1 mark

because the mirro would reflect them

(d) While playing, the children notice a rainbow in the sky.
Rainbows are formed from sunlight and raindrops.
What happens to the sunlight to form a rainbow ?

1 mark

the sun reflecting off the puddles with oil in them and the light reflects up wards multicoloured

maximum 8 marks

2. Mick has a light on his house. When he walks up the path the light comes on. When the light is on at night, Mick forms a shadow on the path.

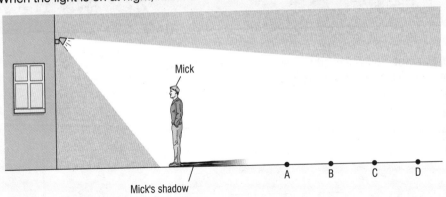

Mick

Mick's shadow

A   B   C   D

(a) (i) Mick's shadow forms as soon as the light comes on.
What does this tell you about the speed of light ?

1 mark

that the speed of light travels Nery fast

(ii) Look at the diagram above. Will the shadow of Mick's head end at A, B, C or D ?

1 mark

_B_

(iii) What will happen to the size of Mick's shadow as he walks towards the house ?

1 mark

Choose the correct answer.   It gets smaller. | A |

It stays the same size. | B |

It gets bigger. | C ✓ |

(b) Inside the light, the bulb fits into a curved surface :

(i) What would the curved surface shown on the diagram look like ?

1 mark

curved surface

bulb

like a ⌀C

(ii) How does the curved surface help the light to work better ?

1 mark

because reflects the light out wards

maximum 5 marks

1. Sunlight is described as white light. It is a mixture of colours.
   These colours can be separated using a prism.

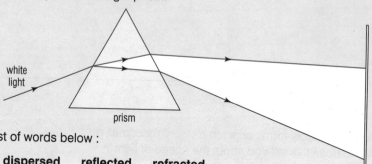

white
light

prism

screen

(a) Look at the list of words below :

   absorbed   **dispersed**   **reflected**   **refracted**

   Which **one** of these words best describes what happens when white light is
   separated into colours ?

   1 mark

(b) Write a letter G on the screen where you would expect to see green light.

   1 mark

(c) (i) Explain why leaves look green in white light.

   1 mark

   _____

   _____

   (ii) What colour would the leaves look in red light ?

   1 mark

   _____

(d) Explain why white light looks green after it has passed through a green filter.

   1 mark

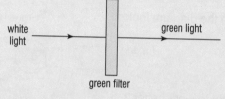

white
light   green light

green filter

_____

_____

   maximum 5 marks

2. (a) Kate has a camera.
The view-finder consists
of two mirrors.
The lower mirror lifts up to
expose the film when Kate
takes a picture.
Kate is going to take a
picture of a bird.

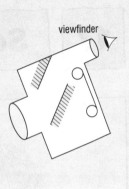

viewfinder

(i) Which bird can she see
in the middle of the
view-finder ?

1 mark

_____

(ii) Use a ruler to draw the
path of a light ray to
show how light from this
bird gets to Kate's eye.

2 marks

(iii) How should Kate move
the camera to see Bird E
in the viewfinder ?

1 mark

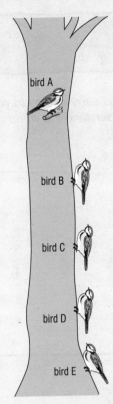

bird A

bird B

bird C

bird D

bird E

_____

(b) When Kate takes a picture, the light passes through the lens and is focused on the
film.

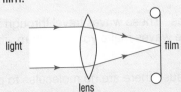

light

lens

film

Which **one** of these words best describes what happens to the light as it passes
through the lens ?

1 mark

reflection	A
dispersion	B
refraction	C
absorption	D

maximum 5 marks

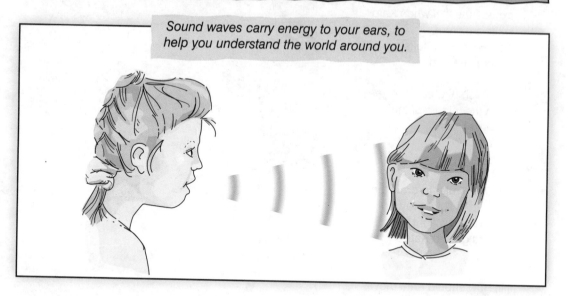

Sound waves carry energy to your ears, to help you understand the world around you.

What you need to know

- Sound travels at about 330 metres per second (in air). Light travels much faster than this.

- Average speed $= \dfrac{\text{distance travelled}}{\text{time taken}}$

- All sounds are caused by vibrations.

- If a guitar string is vibrating, it sends out sound waves. These waves travel through the air to your ear. They transfer energy to your ear. The waves make your ear-drum vibrate and so messages are sent to your brain.

- Sound cannot travel through a vacuum. This is because there are no molecules to pass on the vibrations.

- To compare sound waves you can use a microphone and a CRO (oscilloscope).

- A loud sound has a large amplitude (a) :
  The loudness of a sound is measured in decibels (dB).
  Your ear is easily damaged by loud sounds.

- A high pitch sound has a high frequency :
  The frequency is measured in hertz (Hz).
  The range of frequencies that can be heard varies from person to person.

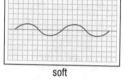

soft

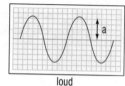

loud

low pitch

high pitch

Useful Words

wave   energy   vibration

amplitude   ear-drum

vacuum   frequency   hertz

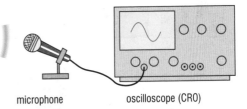

microphone   oscilloscope (CRO)

QuickTest ....

▶ A sound _____ [1] can travel through solids, liquids and gases, but it cannot travel through

a _____ [2] .

▶ The _____ [3] of a guitar string sends a sound _____ [4] through the air.

This wave transfers _____ [5] to your _____ [6] .

▶ A loud sound has a large _____ [7] . It has more _____ [8] than a quiet

sound.

A low pitch sound has a low _____ [9] .

The _____ [10] is measured in _____ [11] (Hz).

▶ Sound travels *faster/slower* [12] than light.

This is why we see the lightning *before/after* [13] the thunder.

The speed of sound is 330 m/s. How far will it travel in 10 seconds ? _____ [14] metres

If lightning strikes 660 m away from you, describe what you would observe. _____

_____ [15]

▶ In these wave diagrams,

  a) Which has the largest amplitude ? _____ [16]

  b) Which has the highest frequency ? _____ [17]

  c) Which was the quietest sound ? _____ [18]

  d) Which sound has the lowest pitch ? _____ [19]

  d) Which 2 have the same frequency ? _____ [20]

A

B

C

D

1. Simon is at a pop concert.
   The sound he hears comes from the loudspeakers on the stage.

(a) (i) How does sound get from the loudspeakers to Simon's ears ?

1 mark

_____

   (ii) Which part of Simon's ear detects the sound ?

1 mark

_____

(b) What are the loudspeakers doing to make the sound ?

   Choose the correct answer.   blowing | A |

   flashing | B |

   spinning | C |

   vibrating | D |

(c) Simon moves from the back of the concert hall, to nearer the stage.

   (i) As Simon gets closer to the stage, how does the **loudness** of the music sound to him ?

1 mark

_____

   (ii) As Simon gets closer to the stage, how does the **pitch** of the music sound to him ?

1 mark

maximum 5 marks

2. (a) Complete the following sentence.

1 mark

Sound is produced when an object _____ .

(b) Jessica is the starter for the school athletics competition. She fires a pistol which makes a loud bang at the start of each race.

BANG!

At the side of the field there is a large brick wall.

(i) Each time Jessica fires the pistol, she hears an echo of the bang a short time after. Why is there an echo ?

1 mark

_____

_____

(ii) Why is it important that Jessica holds the pistol at arm's length when she fires it ?

1 mark

_____

(c) A person's audible range is the range of sounds of different pitch which they can hear.

(i) What often happens to a person's audible range as they grow older ?

1 mark

_____

(ii) When bats fly they send out sound waves. However, people cannot hear the sound waves produced by bats. Suggest why this is so.

1 mark

_____

_____

maximum 5 marks

1. (a) Which **one** of the following statements about sound waves is **true** ?

1 mark

sound waves cannot travel through a vacuum A

sound waves travel faster than light waves C

sound waves cannot be reflected B

sound waves cannot travel through water D

(b) Flies are insects. They make a buzzing sound with their wings. Different types of fly make different sounds.

Carol used an oscilloscope to record the sounds made by four different types of fly. Here are her results. The settings on the oscilloscope were the same each time.

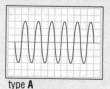 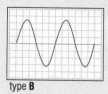 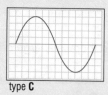 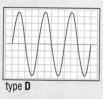

type **A**   type **B**   type **C**   type **D**

(i) Explain how the results show that the flies were making sounds of different pitch.

1 mark

_____

_____

(ii) Explain how the results show that the flies were making sounds of different loudness.

1 mark

_____

_____

(c) Carol recorded the sound made by another fly :

(i) To which type, **A**, **B**, **C** or **D**, does it belong ? _____

1 mark

(ii) Explain your answer.

1 mark

_____

_____

maximum 5 marks

2. Ben watched a storm from his home.

Using his watch Ben found that there were five seconds between seeing a flash of lightning and hearing a clap of thunder.

(a) (i) What effect did the sound of the thunder have on Ben's ear-drums ?

1 mark

_____

(ii) Why did Ben see the lightning before hearing the thunder ?

1 mark

_____

_____

(iii) Sound travels about one kilometre every three seconds.
How far was the storm from Ben's house ?

1 mark

_____

_____

(b) The storm came closer to Ben's house.

(i) How, if at all, did the **amplitude** of the sound of the thunder change ?

1 mark

_____

(ii) How, if at all, did the **frequency** of the sound of the thunder change ?

1 mark

_____

maximum 5 marks

18 Forces

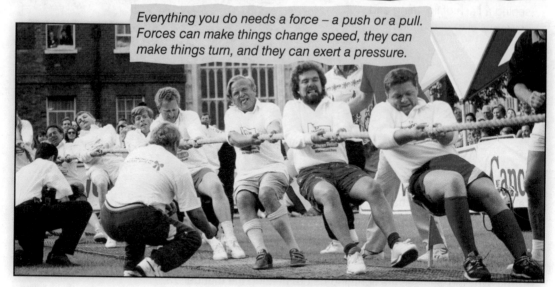

> Everything you do needs a force – a push or a pull.
> Forces can make things change speed, they can
> make things turn, and they can exert a pressure.

What you need to know

- Forces are pushes and pulls. They are measured in newtons (N).
  Friction is a force which tries to slow down movement.
  Air resistance can be reduced by streamlining.
  Weight is a force. It is the pull of gravity by the Earth, downwards.

- If 2 forces on an object are equal and opposite, we say they
  are *balanced* forces. In this case there is no resultant force.
  When the forces are balanced, then the movement of the object
  is not changed (it stays still, or stays moving at a steady speed).

2 N ⟵——•——⟶ 2 N

balanced forces

- If the forces on an object are not balanced, there is a resultant force. This resultant force
  makes the object speed up, or slow down, or change direction.

- The speed of a car can be measured in metres per second or kilometres per hour.

  The formula is : Average speed $= \dfrac{\text{distance travelled}}{\text{time taken}}$

- Levers have many uses. A long spanner is easier to turn than a short spanner.
  The moment (or turning effect) of a force $=$ force $\times$ distance of force from the pivot.
  The principle (or law) of moments says :
  In equilibrium,   the anti-clockwise $=$ the clockwise
                              moments   moments

- Pressure is measured in N/cm^2 or N/m^2 (also called a pascal, Pa).

  The formula is : Pressure $= \dfrac{\text{force} \ \ \text{(in newtons)}}{\text{area} \ \ \text{(in cm}^2 \text{ or m}^2)}$

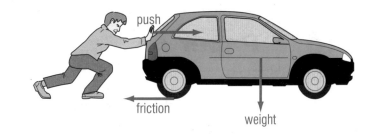

push

friction

weight

QuickTest..

▶ Weight is the force of _____ [1]. It is measured in _____ [2].

Friction is a _____ [3] which always *helps/opposes* [4] the movement of an object.

Air resistance can be reduced by _____ [5] the object.

▶ In the diagram, 2 forces are acting on a block of wood.

These forces are _____ [6], so there is

no _____ [7] force.

If the object was stationary, it will *stay still/start moving* [8].

4 N ←————[ ]————→ 4 N

▶ In the next diagram, the forces are **un**-_____ [9]

and there is a _____ [10] force of _____ [11]

newtons. The block will move to the *left/right* [12].

If the block is moving to the North, a frictional force on it

will act towards the *North/South* [13].

2 N ←————[ ]————→ 5 N

▶ If a car travels 50 km in 2 hours, its speed is _____ [14] km/h.

If a bike moves at 4 m/s for 2 s, it travels _____ [15] metres.

▶ In the diagram, the moment applied by the spanner

is _____ [16] N-cm.

10 N

←— 20 cm —→

▶ A girl stands on one foot. The area of her shoe touching

the floor is 200 cm^2 and her weight is 600 N.

What pressure does she exert on the ground ? _____ [17] N/cm^2.

1. A glider is attached to an aeroplane by a tow rope. The aeroplane pulls the glider to launch it.

glider | tow rope | pull of aeroplane

(a) Before the launch the glider's brakes are on. It does not move. The rope is tight.
   (i) The force of friction prevents the glider from moving.
      In which direction is the force of friction acting ?

      1 mark

   (ii) The aeroplane pulls with a force of 8000 N.
      Which is the correct size of the force of friction acting on the glider ?   *1 mark*

      0 N (zero)　A   8000 N　C

      between 0 N and 8000 N　B   more than 8000 N　D

(b) When the glider's brakes are off, the aeroplane pulls the glider forward.
   The aeroplane pulls with a force of 8000 N.
   As the glider increases speed, what size is the force of friction ?   *1 mark*

   0 N (zero)　A   8000 N　C

   between 0 N and 8000 N　B   more than 8000 N　D

(c) As the glider moves along the runway, the wings receive an upward force from the air.
   The glider weighs 2000 N.
   How big does the upward force have to be before the glider leaves the ground ?
      1 mark
   less than 2000 N　A   2000 N　B   more than 2000 N　C

(d) When the glider has climbed into the air the pilot releases the tow rope. The glider
   slows down. Explain why.

      1 mark

      maximum 5 marks

2. Becky cycles to school. The graph shows the distance travelled at different times during the journey.

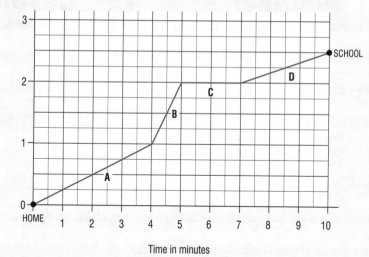

(a) How far is it from Becky's home to school? _____   *1 mark*

(b) During the journey, Becky goes down a steep hill. She also has to stop at a road junction. In which section of the graph, A, B, C or D, does Becky :

(i) go down a steep hill? _____   *1 mark*

(ii) stop at a road junction? _____   *1 mark*

(c) The diagram shows part of the brake on Becky's handlebar.

Becky pulls on the lever with a force of 20 N. What is the force on the cable to the brake?

1 mark

Choose the correct answer.

less than 20 N | A | 20 N | B | more than 20 N | C |

(d) Give **two** ways in which Becky could increase the force pulling the cable.

2 marks

1 _____

2 _____

maximum 6 marks

1. Thrust SSC is a car which held the world
land speed record.
It travels very quickly.

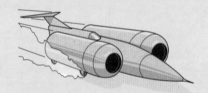

(a) Why does the car have a streamline shape ?

1 mark

_____

(b) The speed of the car is measured by timing how long it takes to travel along a
straight course.
Here are details of three runs. Complete the table.

3 marks

run	distance travelled in m	time taken in s	average speed in m/s
1	1500	6.0	
2	1750		250
3		6.5	240

(c) Why is the value in the last column an *average* speed for a run ?

1 mark

_____

_____

(d) At the end of a run,
a parachute is
released from the
back of the car.

Explain the effect
which the parachute
has on the motion of
the car.   *2 marks*

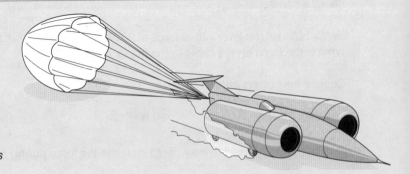

_____

_____

maximum 7 marks

2. The diagram below shows details of a 'hole punch' being used to make holes in leather. When the handle is pulled down the pin is forced into the leather.

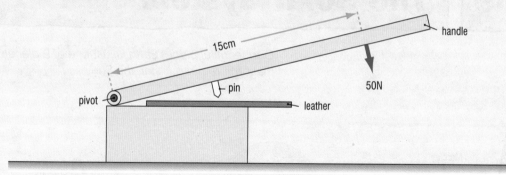

(a) The handle applies a moment, or turning effect, about the pivot.

(i) Calculate the size of this moment (in N cm).

1 mark

_____ N cm

(ii) State **two** ways in which the moment could be increased.

2 marks

1 _____

2 _____

(b) Look at the diagram of part of the hole punch :

The pin is pressed into the leather with a force of 150 N.
The top of the pin has an area of 50 mm².
The point of the pin has an area of 0.1 mm².

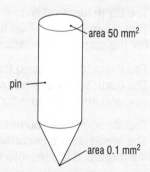

(i) What is the size of the **force** exerted by the point of the pin on the leather ?

1 mark

_____ N

(ii) Calculate the **pressure** exerted by the point of the pin. Give the units.

2 marks

_____

_____

maximum 6 marks

Our beautiful planet Earth is just one of 9 planets that orbit round our star, the Sun.

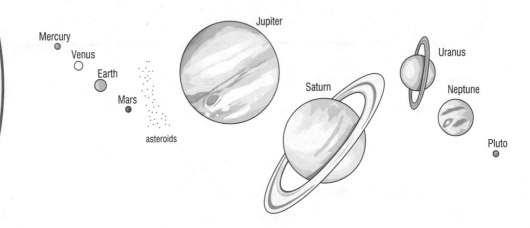

What you need to know..

- The Earth turns on its axis once in 24 hours. This is 1 day.
  This means that the Sun appears to rise in the East and set in the West.
  For the same reason, stars at night appear to move from East to West.

- The Earth travels round the Sun in an orbit, taking 1 year (365¼ days).
  The Earth's axis is tilted (at 23½°). This means that in summer the Sun is higher in the sky, and so day-time is longer and warmer than in winter.

- The Moon moves round the Earth, taking 1 month for a complete orbit.
  The Moon shines because of sunlight on it. It shows different phases at different times of the month. If it goes into the shadow of the Earth, there is an eclipse of the Moon.

- The Sun is a star. It has 9 planets round it. The diagram above shows the order and the relative size of them (but they should be shown much farther apart).

- A planet is held in orbit round the Sun by a gravitational force.
  The shape of each orbit is an ellipse.

- The Sun and other stars are very hot and make their own light.
  The planets and their moons shine only by reflecting the sunlight.

- Artificial satellites and space probes can be launched to observe the Earth and to explore the solar system.

Useful Words

East   West   Sun

planet   Earth

orbit   ellipse

gravitational   star

Spring

Summer
in the UK

Sun

Winter
in the UK

Autumn

The Earth in orbit

QuickTest ....

▶ Each morning the Sun rises in the _____ [1]. It sets in the _____ [2].
At night the stars also appear to move from _____ [3] to _____ [4]. This is because the
_____ [5] is turning.

▶ The Earth takes _____ [6] day (_____ [7] hours) to spin once, and takes _____ [8] year
(_____ [9] days) to travel once round the Sun.

▶ In summer, our part of the _____ [10] is tilted towards the _____ [11], so the Sun
appears *higher/lower* [12] in the sky, and the day-time is *longer/shorter* [13] and *warmer/colder* [14].

▶ There are ____ [15] planets going round the _____ [16]. The biggest one is _____ [17].
The planet between Earth and Jupiter is _____ [18].
The coldest planet is _____ [19]. This is because it is the farthest from the _____ [20].

▶ A planet does not travel in a straight line but in a curved _____ [21] (in the shape of an
_____ [22]). This is because of the _____ [23] force of the
Sun pulling on it.

▶ The Sun is a _____ [24] and makes its own light. A _____ [25] shines only by
reflecting this sunlight, like the Moon.

▶ When a satellite goes round the Earth, it is held in its _____ [26] by the
_____ [27] pull of the _____ [28].

1. (a) How long does it take for the Earth to spin once on its own axis ? *1 mark*

Choose the correct answer.

one day A   one week B   one month C   one year D

(b) The diagram shows the position of the Sun at midday on 21st June.

Draw circles to show the position of the Sun :

    (i) in the morning.
        Label this circle 1. *1 mark*

    (ii) at midday on 21st March.
        Label this circle 2. *1 mark*

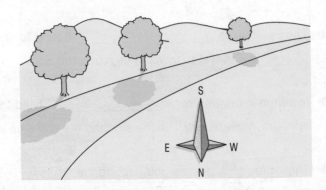

(c) The diagram below shows the position of the Earth on 21st June, and its path around the Sun.

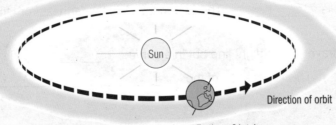

Earth on 21st June

Direction of orbit

    (i) How long does it take the Earth to complete one orbit of the Sun ?

1 mark

_____

    (ii) Draw a circle to show the position of the Earth on 21st December. *1 mark*

maximum 5 marks

2. The diagram shows the position of the Earth in the Solar System.

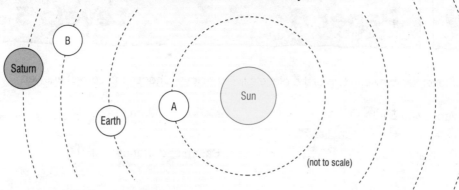

(not to scale)

The other planets in the Solar System are :

Jupiter   Mars   Mercury   Neptune   Pluto   Uranus   Venus

(a) Which of these could be :

(i) planet A ? _____

1 mark

(ii) planet B ? _____

1 mark

(b) How long will it take planet B to complete one orbit of the Sun ?

Choose the correct answer.   less than one Earth year   ☐ A

exactly one Earth year   ☐ B

more than one Earth year   ☐ C

(c) Planets do not produce light, but we can see them. Explain why.

1 mark

_____

(d) When we look at the sky, the position of
planets changes from night to night.
The diagrams show the same part of the night
sky observed at the same time on two nights.

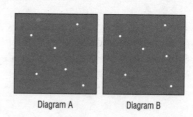

Diagram A   Diagram B

One of the objects is a planet. Draw a circle
around the planet.   *1 mark*

maximum 5 marks

1. (a) Jupiter lies between two of the planets listed below. Choose the correct answer. *1 mark*

   Venus and Earth ☐ A   Mars and Saturn ☐ C

   Earth and Mars ☐ B   Saturn and Uranus ☐ D

   Io and Callisto are two of the moons
   of Jupiter. They are similar in mass.

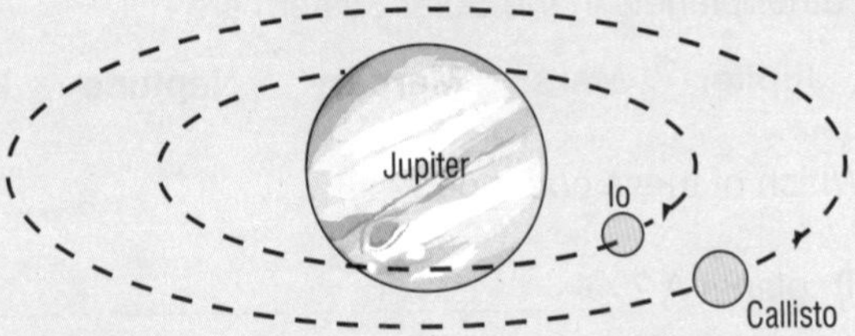

   (b) Which moon is pulled towards
       Jupiter with the greater force ?
       Explain your answer.   *1 mark*

   _____

   _____

   (c) Which moon is moving around Jupiter more quickly ?
       Explain your answer.

       1 mark

   _____

   _____

   (d) In 1995 the artificial satellite Galileo entered the atmosphere of Jupiter. As the satellite
       approached Jupiter, the gravitational force on it changed. Describe the change.

       1 mark

   _____

   _____

   (e) The Earth's Moon has an almost circular orbit around the Earth.
       Apart from Io and Callisto, Jupiter has other moons in orbit around it.
       Suggest why the orbits of Jupiter's moons are not smooth circles.

       1 mark

   _____

   _____

   maximum 5 marks

2. (a) The diagram shows some positions of the Earth relative to the Sun.

Which of these shows the position of the Earth during :

(i) summer in Britain ? _____

1 mark

(ii) winter in Britain ? _____

1 mark

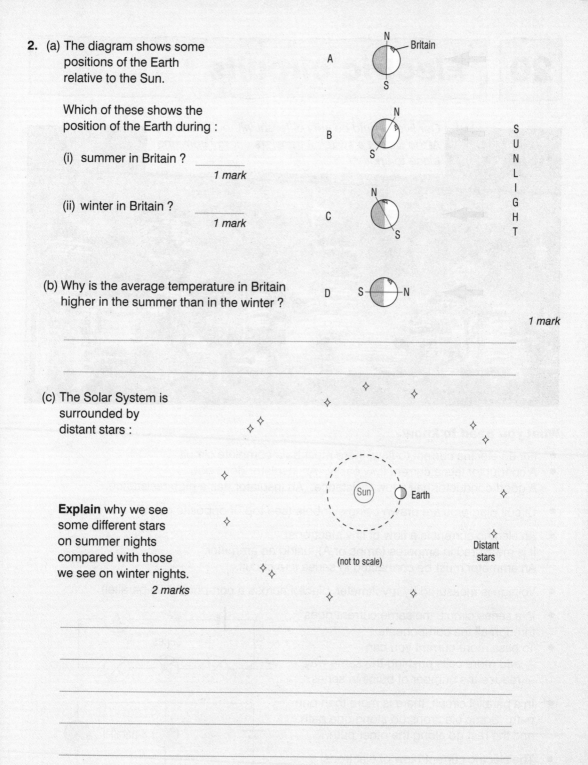

SUNLIGHT

(b) Why is the average temperature in Britain higher in the summer than in the winter ?

1 mark

_____

_____

(c) The Solar System is surrounded by distant stars :

Explain why we see some different stars on summer nights compared with those we see on winter nights.

2 marks

(not to scale)

Distant stars

_____

_____

_____

_____

maximum 5 marks

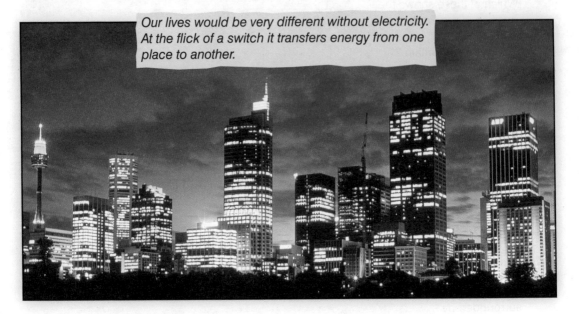

Our lives would be very different without electricity. At the flick of a switch it transfers energy from one place to another.

What you need to know

- For an electric current to flow, there must be a complete circuit.
- A conductor lets a current flow easily. An insulator does not.
  A good conductor has a low resistance. An insulator has a high resistance.

- Circuit diagrams are drawn using symbols (see top of opposite page).

- An electric current is a flow of tiny electrons.
  It is measured in amperes (amps or A), using an ammeter.
  An ammeter must be connected in series in a circuit.

- Voltage is measured by a voltmeter, placed across a component (in parallel).

- In a series circuit, the same current goes through all the components :
- To pass more current you can
  – add more cells pushing the same way,
  – reduce the number of bulbs in series.

- In a parallel circuit, there is more than one path. Some electrons go along one path and the rest go along the other path.

- The electric current (flow of electrons) transfers energy from the cell to the bulbs.

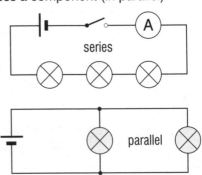

Useful Words

conductor   insulator

current   circuit

series   parallel

circuit symbols

2 cells
(battery)   switch   bulb   ammeter   voltmeter

QuickTest ....

▶ Before an electric _____ ¹ can flow, there must be a complete _____ ²,

with no gaps in it.

A current can flow easily through a _____ ³, but not through an

_____ ⁴.

A current is measured in _____ ⁵ using an _____ ⁶.

A voltage is measured in _____ ⁷ using a _____ ⁸.

▶ In a _____ ⁹ circuit, the _____ ¹⁰

is the same in every part of the circuit.

In the circuit shown here, the components are all

in _____ ¹¹.

If the current through the ammeter is 2 A, what is

the current through bulb X ? _____ ¹².

What is the current through bulb Y ? _____ ¹³.

If you reduced the number of bulbs in the circuit,

the current would be *more/less* ¹⁴.

If you reduced the number of cells, the current

would be *more/less* ¹⁵.

▶ In this circuit, are the bulbs in series or in parallel ?

_____ ¹⁶

Both bulbs are lit. Explain what happens when the

switch is closed. _____

_____ ¹⁷

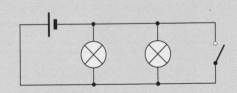

1. Emma has made some electric circuits using cells and bulbs :

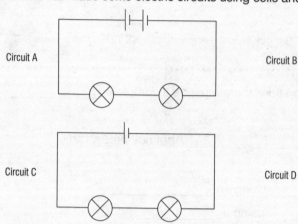

Circuit A

Circuit B

Circuit C

Circuit D

In circuit A the bulbs are lit up, but not very brightly.

(a) Compare the brightness of the bulbs in circuits B, C and D with that in circuit A. Choose your answer from the list below.   *3 marks*

    are out (off)   **are dimmer**   **stay the same**   **are brighter**

    (i) In circuit B the bulbs   _____

    (ii) In circuit C the bulbs   _____

    (iii) In circuit D the bulbs   _____

(b) In which of the circuits, A, B, C or D are the bulbs connected in parallel ?

                                                              1 mark

    _____

(c) Emma placed some ammeters in the circuit shown here to measure the current at different parts of the circuit.

    How much current was recorded by A_2 and A_4 ?
                                       2 marks

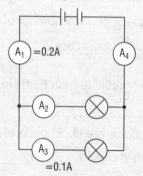

$A_1 = 0.2A$ A_4

A_2

A_3
$= 0.1A$

    $A_2 =$ _____ $A_4 =$ _____

                                                              maximum 6 marks

2. Ayesha has made a circuit containing a bulb, a buzzer and four switches. At the start of her experiment all of the switches are open.

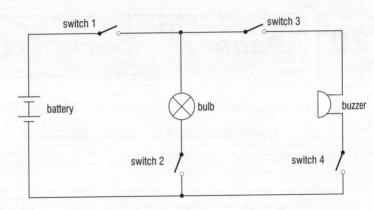

(a) Ayesha closes the switches in this order, first Switch 1, then 2, then 3, and then 4.

   Complete these sentences :

   (i) The bulb will light up after closing switch _____ .   1 mark

   (ii) The buzzer will sound after closing switch _____ .   1 mark

(b) Ayesha took out one of the cells from the battery. Then she joined up the circuit again :

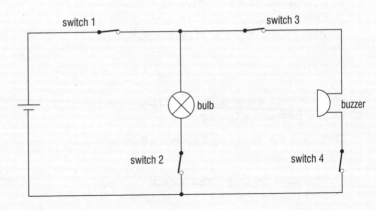

   What effect, if any, does this have on :
                                                                                  1 mark
   (i) the brightness of the bulb ? _____

   (ii) the loudness of the buzzer ? _____   1 mark

(c) Ayesha wants to measure the current in the buzzer. She replaces one of the switches with an ammeter.

   Which of the switches could she change for an ammeter ?
                                                                                  1 mark

   _____

                                                              maximum 5 marks

1. (a) Complete the sentence below using one of the following words.   *1 mark*

         electrons   **atoms**   **cells**   **molecules**

   Electricity is carried through a conductor by _____

(b) The diagram shows a circuit :
The switch is open.

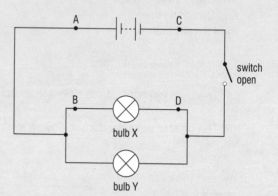

    (i) Chris connects point A to point B
with a thick copper wire.
Which bulbs, if any, will light up ?

                         1 mark

    _____

    (ii) Chris removes the copper wire and
uses it to connect point C to point D.
Which bulbs, if any, light up ?   *1 mark*

    _____

(c) Chris removes the wire and closes the
switch. Both bulbs light up.

   Chris uses the wire to connect point B
to point D, as shown :

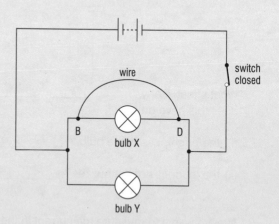

    (i) How does the brightness of each
bulb change, if at all ?   *2 marks*

    Bulb X

    _____

    Bulb Y

    _____

    (ii) The switch is replaced by an ammeter.
How would the reading on the ammeter change, if at all,
when point B was connected to point D ?

                                                  1 mark

    _____

                                       maximum 6 marks

2. (a) In a circuit two bulbs are connected in series.

Which **one** of the following statements about the current in the circuit is true ?   *1 mark*

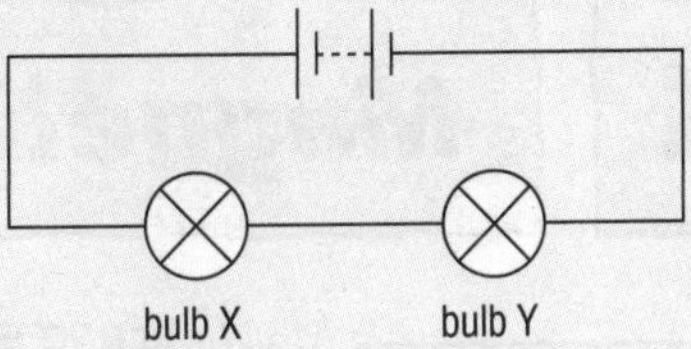

All of the current is used up by bulb X.   **A**

All of the current is used up by bulb Y.   **B**

Half of the current is used up by bulb X and the other half by bulb Y.   **C**

The current is not used up by the bulbs.   **D**

(b) In an experiment you are given two cells and three bulbs. In the circuits you make, you must use all of the components and all of the bulbs must be lit.
Draw diagrams to show how the components should be connected so that :

(i) the three bulbs light as brightly as possible ;   *1 mark*

(ii) the three bulbs light as dimly as possible ;   *1 mark*

(iii) one bulb lights with a different brightness to the other two.   *1 mark*

(c) In which of your circuits, (b)(i) or (b)(ii) would the bulbs would remain lit the longer ? Explain why.   *1 mark*

_____

_____

maximum 5 marks

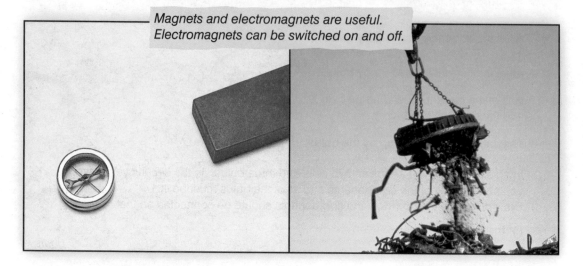

Magnets and electromagnets are useful.
Electromagnets can be switched on and off.

What you need to know

- The end of a compass that points North
  is called the North pole (N-pole) of the magnet.
- Two N-poles (or two S-poles) repel each other.
  An N-pole attracts an S-pole.

- Iron and steel can be magnetised.

- You can find the shape of the magnetic field
  around a bar magnet by using iron filings
  (or small plotting compasses).

- The Earth has a magnetic field around it.
  A compass points along the field.

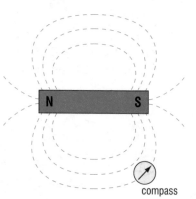

compass

- A current in a coil produces a magnetic field like a bar magnet.
  It is an electromagnet (see opposite page).
- The strength of an electromagnet depends on:
  (1) the current in the coil,
  (2) the number of turns on the coil, and
  (3) whether there is an iron core.
  Reversing the current, reverses the North and South poles.

- In a relay, a small current in the coil of an electromagnet is used to switch on
  a bigger current.

- In an electric bell, an electromagnet is used to attract an iron bar so that it
  breaks the circuit repeatedly. The vibrating iron bar makes the bell ring.

Useful Words

compass   iron   repel   attract

bar   current   circuit   field

magnet   N-pole   S-pole   core

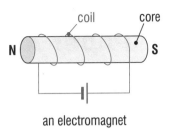

an electromagnet

QuickTest...

▶ Iron and steel can be magnetised by a _____ [1] or an electromagnet.
   Two N-poles _____ [2] each other. Two S-poles _____ [3] each other.
   An N-pole _____ [4] an S-pole.

▶ The shape of the magnetic field around an electromagnet
   is the same shape as the field around a _____ [5] magnet.
   We can see the shape using _____ [6] filings or a _____ [7].

▶ An electromagnet can be made stronger by :
   – *increasing/decreasing* [8] the current in the coil,
   – *increasing/decreasing* [9] the number of turns on the coil,
   – *adding/removing* [10] an iron core.

▶ In the diagram, an iron bar is hanging from a string,
   near a coil.
   When the switch is pressed, a _____ [11]
   flows round the _____ [12], and the coil
   becomes an _____ [13].
   It now has a magnetic _____ [14] round it. This field
   will be stronger if the coil has an iron _____ [15].
   The electromagnet now _____ [16] the
   iron bar, which hits the bell.
   What happens when the switch is opened ?

   _____
                                    [17]
   _____

1.

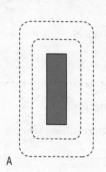 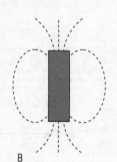  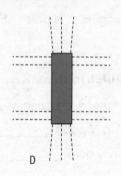

A   B   C   D

(a) Which diagram best shows the shape of the magnetic field
    around a bar magnet ? Choose the correct letter.

1 mark

(b) Laura used a magnet to pick up a metal bar. A nail stuck to
    the other end of this metal bar at point Y, as shown :

    (i) From which element could the metal bar be made ?

1 mark

_____

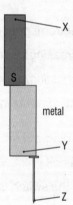

    (ii) What are the magnetic poles at points X, Y and Z ?
         Point X has been done for you in the table.

2 marks

point	N pole	S pole	no magnetic pole
X	✔		
Y			
Z			

(iii) When Laura took the magnet away from the metal bar, the nail fell off.
      Explain why.

1 mark

_____

_____

maximum 5 marks

2. Tom has two bar magnets. The poles are marked on one of the magnets, but not on the other.

(a) Tom wants to identify both poles on magnet B. Describe an experiment Tom could carry out to do this, using only the two magnets.

2 marks

_____

_____

_____

(b) Tom built a circuit containing a reed switch. This switch has two iron reeds in it.

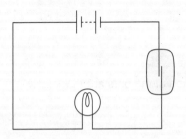 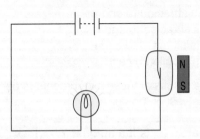

(i) What happened when Tom placed a magnet next to the reed switch ?

1 mark

_____

(ii) Explain why this happened.

1 mark

_____

_____

(c) The diagram shows what happened when Tom placed a coil of wire carrying a current around the reed switch :

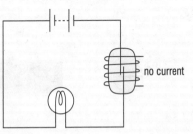 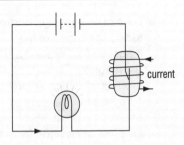

Explain why this happened.

1 mark

_____

_____

maximum 5 marks

1. (a) Luke has three iron bars, each of which may be a bar magnet.

(i) He carried out some experiments and found the following :

End **s** is attracted to end **p**.
End **t** is attracted to end **r**.
End **o** is attracted to end **r**.
End **r** is repelled by end **s**.

Use the results of these experiments to decide which of the bars are magnets.
Answer 'yes' or 'no' for each bar.

3 marks

bar	is it a magnet ?
o — p	
q — r	
s — t	

(ii) Suggest another way in which Luke could decide which of the bars were magnetic.

1 mark

_____

(b) Luke uses a plotting compass
to find the shape of the
magnetic field around a
bar magnet.
In which direction will the
compass needle point at
each of the positions shown ?
One has been done for you.

2 marks

(c) The pointed end of a compass needle is a magnetic north pole. It always points north.
What does this tell you about the magnetic polarity of the Earth's North Pole ?

1 mark

_____

maximum 7 marks

2. The diagram shows an electromagnet. It is made by wrapping a coil of wire around a soft iron core.

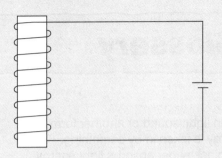

(a) (i) State **one** way in which the strength of this electro-magnet could be increased.

1 mark

_____

(ii) Briefly describe a simple experiment you could carry out to show that the strength of the electromagnet had increased.

1 mark

_____

_____

_____

(b) The diagram shows details of a relay switch which contains an electromagnet.

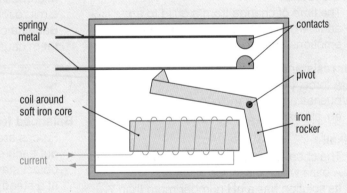

(i) What happens when an electric current is passed through the coil ?

1 mark

_____

(ii) Why is the coil wrapped around a soft iron core ?

1 mark

_____

(iii) Explain why iron is a good choice of material for the rocker.

1 mark

_____

_____

maximum 5 marks

Glossary

Absorb
When light, sound or another form of energy is taken in by something.
eg. black paper absorbs light energy.

Acid
A sour substance which can attack metal, clothing or skin.
The chemical opposite of an alkali.
When dissolved in water its solution has a pH number less than 7.

Adaptation
A feature that helps a plant or an animal to survive in changing conditions.

Adolescence
The time of change from a child to an adult, when both our bodies and our emotions change.

Air resistance
A force, due to friction with the air, which pushes against a moving object.
eg. air resistance slows down a parachute.

Alkali
The chemical opposite of an acid.
A base which dissolves in water.
Its solution has a pH number more than 7.

Amplitude
The size of a vibration or wave, measured from its midpoint.
A loud sound has a large amplitude.

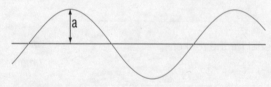

Antibiotic
A useful drug that helps your body fight a disease.

Atom
The smallest part of an element. All atoms contain protons and electrons.

Atomic number
The number of protons in each atom of the element.
Elements are arranged in the periodic table in order of this atomic number.

Axis
The Earth spins on its axis. It is an imaginary line passing through the Earth from the North Pole to the South Pole.

Bacteria
Microbes made up of one cell, visible with a microscope.
Bacteria can grow quickly and some of them cause disease. eg. pneumonia.

Balanced forces
Forces are balanced when they cancel out each other (see page 108). The object stays still, or continues to move at a steady speed in a straight line.

Base
The oxide, hydroxide or carbonate of a metal. (If a base dissolves in water it is called an *alkali*).

Biomass Fuel
Fuel (eg. wood) made from growing plants.

Boiling point
The temperature at which a liquid boils and changes into a gas.

Braking distance
The distance a car travels *after* the brake is pressed.

Capillaries
Tiny blood vessels that let substances like oxygen, food and carbon dioxide pass into and out of the blood.

Carbohydrate
Your body's fuel. Food like glucose that gives you your energy.

Carnivores
Animals that eat only other animals – meat eaters.

Cell membrane
The structure that surrounds a cell and controls what goes in and out.

Cell wall
The strong layer on the outside of a plant cell that supports the cell.

Cells
The 'building blocks' of life.
They are made up of a *cell membrane, cytoplasm* and *nucleus.*

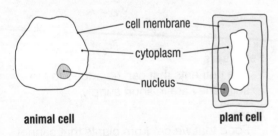

cell membrane

cytoplasm

nucleus

animal cell   **plant cell**

Chemical change
A change which makes a new substance. eg. coal burning.

Chlorophyll
A green chemical in plants used to trap light energy for photosynthesis.

Chloroplasts
Tiny, round structures found inside plant cells. They capture light energy and use it to make food in photosynthesis.

Chromatography
A method used to separate mixtures of substances, usually coloured.

Combustion
The reaction which occurs when a substance burns in oxygen, giving out heat energy.

Competition
A struggle for survival. Living things compete for scarce resources. eg. space.

Component
One of the parts that make up an electric circuit. eg. battery, switch, bulb:

Compound
A substance made when two or more elements are chemically joined together. eg. water is a compound made from hydrogen and oxygen.

Conductor
An electrical conductor allows a current to flow through it.
A thermal conductor allows heat energy to pass through it.
All metals are good conductors.

Cytoplasm
The jelly-like part of the cell where many chemical reactions take place.

Density
A measure of how heavy something is for its size:
$$\text{density} = \frac{\text{mass}}{\text{volume}}$$

Diffusion
The process of particles moving and mixing of their own accord, without being stirred or shaken.

Digestion
Breaking down food so that it is small enough to pass through the gut into the blood.

Dispersion
The splitting of a beam of white light into the 7 colours of the spectrum, by passing it through a glass prism.

Distillation

A way to separate a liquid from a mixture of liquids, by boiling off the substances at different temperatures.

Drug

A chemical that alters the way in which your body works.
eg. alcohol, cannabis, nicotine, solvents.

Egestion

Getting rid of indigestible food from the gut.

Electric current

A flow of electric charges (electrons). It is measured in amps (A) by an ammeter.

Electromagnet

A coil of wire becomes a magnet when a current flows through it. See page 127.

Electron

A tiny particle with a negative charge.

Element

A substance that is made of only one type of atom.

Embryo

The fertilised egg grows into an embryo and eventually into a baby.

Endothermic

A reaction that *takes in* heat energy from the surroundings.

Energy transfer

See *Transfer of energy.*

Enzymes

Chemicals that act like catalysts to speed up digestion of our food.

Equation

A shorthand way of showing the changes that take place in a chemical reaction.

eg. iron + sulphur ⟶ iron sulphide

Fe + S ⟶ FeS

Equilibrium

A balanced situation, when all the forces cancel out each other.

Erosion

The wearing away of rocks.

Exothermic

A reaction that *gives out* heat energy to the surroundings.

Fat

Food used as a store of energy and to insulate our bodies so we lose less heat.

Fermentation

The reaction when sugar is turned into alcohol.

Fertilisation

When sex cells join together to make a new individual.
eg. a sperm and an egg, or a pollen grain nucleus and an ovule nucleus.

Fertilisers

The nutrients that can be added to the soil if they are in short supply.

Fibre

Food that we get from plants that cannot be digested. It gives the gut muscles something to push against.

Filtration

A process used to separate undissolved solids from liquids.

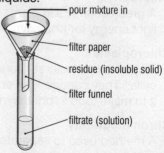

pour mixture in
filter paper
residue (insoluble solid)
filter funnel
filtrate (solution)

Flowers
The organs that many plants use to reproduce by making seeds.

Food chain
A diagram that shows how food energy is passed between plants and animals.

Food web
A diagram that shows a number of food chains linked together.

Formula
A combination of symbols to show the elements which a compound contains. eg. MgO is the formula for magnesium oxide.

Fossil
The remains of an animal or plant which have been preserved in rocks.

Fossil fuels
A fuel made from the remains of plants and animals that died millions of years ago. eg. coal, oil, natural gas.

Frequency
The number of complete vibrations in each second. A sound with a high frequency has a high pitch.

Friction
A force when two surfaces rub together. It always pushes against the movement.

Fuel
A substance that is burned in air (oxygen) to give out energy.

Gas
A substance which is light, has the shape of its container and is easily squashed. The particles in a gas are far apart. They move quickly and in all directions.

Gravity, gravitational force
A force of attraction between 2 objects. The pull of gravity on you is your weight.

Group
All the elements in one column down the periodic table.

Habitat
The place where a plant or animal lives.

Herbivores
Animals that eat only plants.

Igneous rock
A rock formed by molten (melted) material cooling down.

Image
When you look in a mirror, you see an image of yourself.

Immune
Not being able to catch a particular disease because you have the antibodies in your blood to fight it.

Inherited
The features that are passed on from parents to their offspring.

Insulator
An electrical insulator does not allow a current to flow easily.
A thermal insulator does not let heat energy flow easily.

Joint
The point where two bones meet. Joints usually allow movement.

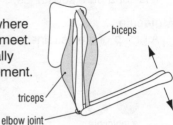

biceps

triceps

elbow joint

Kinetic energy
The energy of something which is moving.

Law of reflection
When light rays bounce off a mirror:
angle of incidence = angle of reflection

Liquid

A substance which has the shape of its container, can be poured and is not easily squashed. The particles in a liquid are quite close together but free to move.

Lungs

The organs in our body that collect oxygen and get rid of carbon dioxide.

Magma

Hot molten rock below the Earth's surface.

Magnetic field

The area round a magnet where it attracts or repels another magnet.

Magnetic material

A substance which is attracted by a magnet. eg. iron and steel.

Melting point

The temperature at which a solid melts and changes into a liquid.

Metal

An element which is a good conductor and is usually shiny. eg. copper.

Metamorphic rock

A rock formed by heating and compressing (squeezing) an existing rock.

Mixture

A substance made when some elements or compounds are mixed together. It is *not* a pure substance.

Molecule

A group of atoms joined together.

a molecule of water, H_2O

oxygen atom

hydrogen atom

Moment

The turning effect of a force.

Moment = force × distance from the pivot.

Muscle

Structures that contract and relax to move bones at joints.

Neutral

Something which is neither an acid nor an alkali.

Neutralisation

The chemical reaction of an acid with a base, in which they cancel each other out.

Non-Metal

An element which does not conduct electricity. (The exception to this is graphite – a form of carbon which is a non-metal, but does conduct).

Non-renewable resources

Energy sources that are used up and not replaced. eg. fossil fuels.

Nucleus of an atom

The centre of an atom.

Nucleus of a cell

A round structure that controls the cell and contains the instructions to make more cells.

Nutrients

The chemicals needed by plants for healthy growth. eg. nitrates, phosphates.

Omnivores

Animals that eat both plants and animals.

Orbit

The path of a planet or a satellite. Its shape is usually an ellipse (oval).

ellipse

Organ

A structure made up of different tissues that work together to do a particular job.

Organism

A living thing such as a plant, an animal or a microbe.

Ovary
Where the eggs are made in a female.

Oxidation
The reaction when oxygen is added to a substance.

Parallel circuit
A way of connecting things in an electric circuit, so that the current divides and passes through different branches. See page 120.

Period (1)
When the lining of the uterus breaks down and blood and cells leave the body through the vagina.

Period (2)
All the elements in one row across the periodic table.

Periodic table
An arrangement of elements in the order of their atomic numbers, forming groups and periods.

pH number
A number which shows how strong the acid or alkali is.
Acids have pH 1–6. (pH1 is very strong)
Alkalis have pH 8–14. (pH 14 is very strong)

Photosynthesis
The process by which green plants use light energy to turn carbon dioxide and water into sugars:

$$\text{carbon dioxide} + \text{water} \xrightarrow{\text{light and chlorophyll}} \text{sugar} + \text{oxygen}$$

Physical change
A change in which no new substance is made. The substance just changes to a different state. eg. water boiling.

Pitch
A whistle has a high pitch and a bass guitar has a low pitch.

Placenta
A structure that forms in the uterus allowing the blood of the baby and the blood of the mother to come close together.

Pollination
The transfer of pollen from the anthers to the stigma of a flower.

Population
A group of animals or plants of the same species living in the same habitat.

Potential Energy
Stored energy. eg. a bike at the top of a hill.

Pressure
A large force pressing on a small area gives a high pressure.
$$\text{Pressure} = \frac{\text{force}}{\text{area}}$$

Principle of conservation of energy
The amount of energy before a transfer is always equal to the amount of energy after the transfer. The energy is 'conserved'.

Producers
Green plants that make their own food by photosynthesis.

Product
A substance made as a result of a chemical reaction.

Protein
Food needed for the growth and repair of cells.

Proton
A tiny positive particle inside the nucleus of an atom.

Pyramid of numbers
A diagram to show how many living things there are at each level in a food chain.

top carnivore
carnivore
herbivore
producer

Reaction

A chemical change which makes a new substance.

reactants $\xrightarrow{\text{reaction}}$ products

Reactivity series

A list of elements in order of their reactivity. The most reactive element is put at the top of the list.

Reduction

A reaction when oxygen is removed. eg. copper oxide is reduced to copper.

Refraction

A ray of light passing from one substance into another is bent (refracted).

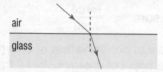

Relay

A switch that is operated by an electro-magnet. A small current can switch on a large current.

Renewable energy resources

Energy sources that do not get used up. eg. solar energy, wind, waves, tides, etc.

Resistance

A thin wire gives more resistance to an electric current than a thick wire.

Respiration

The release of energy from food in our cells. Usually using up oxygen and producing carbon dioxide.

glucose + oxygen $\longrightarrow$ carbon dioxide + water + energy

Resultant force

The result of *unbalanced forces*. See p 109.

Rock cycle

A cycle that means that one type of rock can be changed into another type of rock over a period of time.

Salt

A substance made when an acid and a base react together.

Satellite

An object that goes round a planet or a star. eg. the Moon round the Earth.

Saturated solution

A solution in which no more solid can dissolve at that temperature.

Scattering

When rays of light hit a rough surface (like paper) they reflect off in all directions.

Sedimentary Rock

A rock formed by squashing together layers of material that settle out in water.

Selective breeding

Choosing which animals and plants to breed in order to pass on useful features to the offspring. eg. high milk yield.

Series circuit

A way of connecting things in an electric circuit, so that the current flows through each one in turn. See page 120.

Solar System

The sun and all 9 planets that go round it.

Solid

A substance which has a fixed shape, is not runny and is not easily squashed. The particles in a solid are packed very closely together - they vibrate but do not move from place to place.

Soluble

Describes something which dissolves. eg. salt is soluble in water.

Solute

The solid that dissolves to make a solution.

Solution

The clear liquid made when a solute dissolves in a solvent. eg. salt (solute) dissolves in water (solvent) to make salt solution.

Solvent
The liquid that dissolves the solute to make a solution.

Spectrum
The colours of the rainbow that can be separated when white light is passed through a prism: red, orange, yellow, green, blue, indigo, violet (ROY G. BIV).

Speed
How fast an object is moving.
$$\text{Speed} = \frac{\text{distance travelled}}{\text{time taken}}$$

States of Matter
The 3 states in which matter can be found: solid, liquid and gas.

Temperature
How hot or cold something is.
It is measured in °C, using a thermometer.

Testis
Where the sperms are made in a male.

Thermal energy
Another name for heat energy.

Thermal transfer
When a cup of tea cools down, there is a transfer of thermal energy (heat) from the cup to the surroundings.
This transfer can be by conduction, convection, radiation and evaporation.

Thinking distance
The distance travelled in a car during the driver's reaction time.

Tissue
A group of similar cells that look the same and do the same job.

Transfer of energy
The movement of energy from one place to another, for a job to be done.

Transformation of energy
When energy changes from one form to another.
eg. when paper burns, chemical energy is changed to heat and light energy.

Unbalanced forces
If 2 forces do not cancel out each other, they are unbalanced. There will be a resultant force. See page 109.
The object will change its speed or change its direction

See page 109.

Universal indicator
A liquid which changes colour when acids or alkalis are added to it. It shows whether the acid or alkali is strong or weak.

Uterus
The womb, where a fertilised egg settles and grows into a baby.

Variation
Differences between *different* species (eg. between dogs and cats), or between individuals of the *same* species (eg. people in your class).

Vibrating
Moving backwards and forwards quickly.

Viruses
Extremely small microbes which are not visible with a microscope. Many spread disease by invading cells and copying themselves. eg. influenza.

Vitamins
Complex chemicals needed in small amounts to keep us healthy. eg. vitamin C

Wavelength
The distance between 2 peaks of a wave:

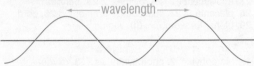

Weathering
The crumbling away of rocks caused by weather conditions such as wind and rain.

QuickTest Answers

1. Cells   page 7
1. membrane   2. cytoplasm   3. nucleus
4. sperm   5. tail   6. root hair   7. absorb   8. cilia
9. palisade   10. chloroplasts   11. cell wall   12. egg
13. tissues   14. organism
15. viruses   16. antibodies   17. immunity
18. antibiotics

2. Food and digestion   page 13
1. balanced (or healthy)   2., 3. carbohydrates, fats
4. respiration   5. proteins   6., 7. vitamins, minerals
8. fibre (or roughage)
9. insoluble   10. digestion   11. enzymes
12. enzymes   13. digestion   14. gut   15. blood
16. gut   17. egestion
18., 19. alcohol, solvents
20. gullet (or oesophagus)   21. stomach
22. small intestine   23. large intestine   24. liver
25. pancreas   26. anus

3. The active body   page 19
1. respiration   2. energy   3. oxygen
4. carbon dioxide   5. respiration
6. lungs   7. wind-pipe (or trachea)   8. oxygen
9. blood   10. carbon dioxide
11. blood   12. oxygen   13. carbon dioxide
14. lungs   15. blood   16. food   17. kidneys
18., 19. cancer, bronchitis
20. skeleton   21. protects   22. bones   23.contracts
24. antagonistic
25. food   26. oxygen   27. carbon dioxide
28. food   29. oxygen
30. carbon dioxide

4. Growing up   page 25
1. testes   2. sperm tube   3. semen   4. ovaries
5. egg tube (or Fallopian tube)   6. uterus (or womb)
7. vagina   8. fertilisation   9. egg tube (or Fallopian tube)   10. egg tube (or Fallopian tube)
11. uterus (or womb)   12. embryo
13. placenta   14. placenta   15. placenta   16. cord
17. fluid sac (or amnion)   18. uterus (or womb)
19. vagina   20. period (or menstruation)
21. adolescence   22. testes
23. adolescence   24. ovaries   25. periods
26. placenta   27. fluid sac (or amnion)   28. cord
29. uterus (or womb)   30. vagina

5. Plants at work   page 31
1. chlorophyll   2. photosynthesis   3. oxygen
4. photosynthesis   5. carbon dioxide
6. oxygen   7. respiration   8. oxygen   9. respiration
10. photosynthesis   11. carbon dioxide
12. respiration

13. carbon dioxide   14. nutrients (or minerals)
15. nitrates   16. nutrients (or minerals)
17. nutrients (or minerals)   18. fertilisers
19. nutrients (or minerals)   20. root hairs
21. pollen   22. ovules   23. pollen   24. pollination
25. pollen   26. ovule   27. fertilisation
28. fertilisation   29. fruit   30. ovule

6. Variation   page 37
1. species   2. similar
3. parents   4. inherit   5. environmental
6., 7., 8., 9. blood group, height, brown eyes, freckles
10. classifying
11. birds   12. worms   13. conifers   14. fish
15. insects   16. molluscs   17. mosses
18. selective   19. yield   20. selective
21. segmented worms   22. starfish group
23. arthropod/arachnid   24. mollusc
25. jellyfish group

7. Environment   page 43
1. habitat   2. adaptations   3. seeds   4. hibernate
5. migrate
6. population   7. limit   8., 9. food, space, climate
10. prey   11. compete   12. food
13. territory, space, food
14., 15. light, space (or nutrients)   16. seeds
17. producers   18., 19. blackbirds, ladybirds, ground
beetles   20. rise   21. fall   22. garden plants
23. ground beetles   24. blackbirds   25. blackbirds
26.

blackbirds
ground beetles
snails
garden plants

8. Matter   page 49
1. liquids   2. solids   3. matter   4. particles
5. vibrate   6. expands   7. contraction
8. diffusion   9. gases
10. melting   11. freezes   12. evaporates
13. condensation   14. soluble   15. insoluble
16. solute   17. solvent   18. saturated   19. hotter
20. it is dissolving   21. by heating the water

9. Elements   page 55
1. elements   2. atom   3. symbol
4., 5. metals, non-metals
6. shiny   7. conductor   8. metal   9. aluminium
10. oxygen   11. nitrogen   12. carbon   13. calcium
14., 15. Na, K   16., 17. F, Br   18., 19., 20. Na, Mg, S
21. Na or K   22. Br   23. S   24. Mg

10. Compounds and Mixtures page 61

1. reaction (or change) 2. composition 3. same
4. molecule 5. atoms
6. pure 7. mixture 8. easy
9. chromatography 10. dissolve 11. filter
12. evaporate
13. sea water 14. heat (or Bunsen burner)
15. thermometer 16. condenser 17. water in
18. water out 19. pure water
20. M 21. E 22. M 23. E 24. C 25. C

11. Chemical reactions page 67

1. physical 2. easy 3. chemical 4. difficult
5. mass
6. reactants 7. product
8. exothermic 9. temperature
10. neutralisation 11. combustion 12. reduction
13. thermal decomposition 14. fermentation
15. calcium oxide 16. chlorine 17. iron sulphide
18. B 19. A 20. C

12. Rocks page 73

1. expand 2. contract 3. weathering 4. freezes
5. acid rain 6. igneous 7. small 8. larger
9. sedimentary 10. metamorphic
11. erosion 12. rocks transported
13. rocks deposited 14. new rocks formed

13. The Reactivity Series page 79

1. metals 2. Reactivity Series
3. reactive 4. hydrogen 5. displaces
6. hydrogen 7. hydrogen 8. calcium oxide
9., 10. magnesium sulphate, copper 11., 12. (No
reaction) tin, zinc chloride 13., 14. zinc oxide, copper
15. X 16. Z 17. Y
18. A 19. C 20. B 21. bubbles of hydrogen gas
given off more quickly with more reactive metal

14. Acids and alkalis page 85

1. pH 2. universal indicator 3. bases 4. salts
5. chloride 6. nitrate
7. acid 8. neutralisation 9. alkali
10. blue/purple 11. B 12. A 13. C
14. bubbles of hydrogen gas (or fizzing)
15. bubbles of carbon dioxide gas (or fizzing)
16., 17. sodium sulphate, water
18., 19., 20. copper chloride, carbon dioxide, water.

15. Energy page 91

1. kinetic 2. potential 3., 4. coal, oil
5. non-renewable 6. Sun (sunlight) 7. renewable
8. wind, waves, sunlight (solar energy), hydroelectric
dams, tides, geothermal stations, biomass (eg. plants)
9. thermal (or heat) 10. molecules (or atoms)
11. more 12. energy
13. thermal (or heat or internal)
14. conduction 15. convection
16. transferred 17. kinetic (movement)
18. chemical (or potential or stored) 19. electricity
20., 21. light and thermal (heat) 22. conserved
23. less

16. Light page 97

1. faster 2. reflection 3. incidence 4. reflection
5. 50 cm directly behind the mirror (so that the line
joining the object and image is at right angles to the
mirror)
6. ray (or beam or wave) 7. speed 8. slows down
9. refracted 10. towards 11. refraction 12. away
from 13. prism 14. spectrum (or rainbow)
15. dispersion 16. orange 17. yellow 18. green
19. blue 20. indigo 21. violet
22. blue 23. absorbs 24. red (only) 25. absorbs
26. black (all light absorbed)
27. some rays go past my hand and reach the wall to
make it bright; other rays hit my hand and so do not
reach the wall, leaving it dark

17. Sound page 103

1. wave 2. vacuum
3. vibration 4. wave 5. energy 6. ear-drum
7. amplitude 8. energy (or amplitude, or decibels)
9. frequency 10. frequency 11. hertz
12. slower 13. before 14. 3300
15. see a lightning flash, and then 2 seconds later hear
the thunder 16. A 17. C 18. B 19. D
20. A, B (same wavelength)

18. Forces page 109

1. gravity 2. newtons (N) 3. force 4. opposes
5. streamlining 6. balanced (equal and opposite)
7. resultant 8. stay still 9. (un-) balanced
10. resultant (or unbalanced) 11. 3 12. right
13. south 14. 25 15. 8 16. 200 17. 3

19. The Solar System page 115

1. East 2. West 3. East 4. West 5. Earth
6. one 7. 24 8. one 9. 365 (365$\frac{1}{4}$)
10. Earth (or planet) 11. Sun 12. higher
13. longer 14. warmer 15. 9 16. Sun
17. Jupiter 18. Mars 19. Pluto 20. Sun
21. orbit (or ellipse) 22. ellipse (oval)
23. gravitational 24. star 25. planet
26. orbit 27. gravitational 28. Earth

20. Electric circuits page 121

1. current 2. circuit 3. conductor 4. insulator
5. amperes (amps) 6. ammeter 7. volts
8. voltmeter 9. series 10. current 11. series
12. 2A 13. 2A 14. more 15. less
16. parallel 17. both the bulbs go out, because the
switch has short-circuited them (all the current goes
through the switch, which has less resistance)

21. Magnetism page 127

1. magnet 2. repel 3. repel 4. attracts
5. bar 6. iron 7. compass 8. increasing
9. increasing 10. adding 11. current
12. circuit (or coil) 13. electromagnet 14. field
15. core 16. attracts
17. the current stops, so the coil stops being an
electromagnet, so gravity pulls the iron bar vertical,
as shown on the diagram

Test tips

The national Test is usually in May in Year 9. As the date approaches, make sure you are fully prepared.

In the days before the Test:

- Revise your work carefully. You can use the *'What you need to know'* sections in this book.
- You can also revise by reading again the *QuickTests* and the other test papers, and the answers to them.
  Try to answer the questions before you read the answers.
- Ask your teacher for copies of the Tests from earlier years. Try to do as many as you can, and time yourself.
- On the day of the Test, make sure you take the correct equipment.
  This is usually: pen, pencil, rubber, ruler, protractor and calculator.
  A watch is also useful, so that you can pace yourself in the Test.

In the examination room:

- Read each question carefully. Make sure you understand what the question is about and what you are expected to do.
- How much detail do you need to give? The question gives you clues:
  - Give short answers to questions which start: *'State ...'* or *'List ...'* or *'Name ...'*.
  - Give longer answers if you are asked to *'Explain ...'* or *'Describe ...'* or asked *'Why does ...?'*.
- The number of marks shown on the page usually tells you how many points the examiner is looking for in your answer.
- The number of lines of space is also a guide to how much is needed.
- If you find a question too hard, go on to the next question. But try to write something for each part of every question.
- If you have spare time at the end, use it wisely to check over your answers.

Acknowledgements

Allsport: 18 Elda Hacch; Britstock-IFA: 120 Chris Walsh; Martyn Chillmaid: 78R; Rex Features: 104 Brian Rasic; Robert Harding Picture Library: 12, 54; Science Photolibrary: 78L, 84 Dr J Burgess, 126R,L, 135 Alfred Pasieka, 139 Fred Burrell; Telegraph Colour Library: 96 L Lefkowitz; Tony Stone Images: 24 Ron Sutherland, 36 Lori Adamski Peek, 60 Jean-François Causse, 90 Chad Slattery; Topham Picture Point: 108 Tom Scott/MJB.

Many thanks to Lawrie Ryan, Derek McMonagle, Colin McCarty, Geoff Hardwick and the team at Alsager School, John Bailey, John Hepburn and Adrian Wheaton.

First published 1998 by

Stanley Thornes (Publishers) Ltd, Delta Place, 27 Bath Road, CHELTENHAM GL53 7TH

A catalogue record for this book is available from the British Library.

ISBN 978 0 7487 5528 8

07 08 09 / 10 9 8 7 6 5 4 3

Typeset by Magnet Harlequin, Oxford   Artwork by Peters and Zabransky & Magnet Harlequin   Printed and bound in Spain by Graficas Estella S.A.

Index